PAPERWEIGHT

Echoes of Stardust

Stephen McGill

Published by Lee's Press and Publishing Company
www.LeesPress.net

Lee's PRESS | A Premiere Self-Publishing Services Company

All rights reserved 2024, Except for brief excerpts for review purposes, no part of this book may be reproduced or used in any form without written permission from Stephen McGill and/or the publisher.

This document is published by Lee's Press and Publishing Company located in the United States of America. It is protected by the United States Copyright Act, all applicable state laws, and international copyright laws. The information in this document is accurate to the best of the ability of Stephen McGill at the time of writing. The content of this document is subject to change without notice.

ISBN-13: 978-1-964234-11-3

PAPERBACK

TABLE OF CONTENTS

Acknowledgements 1

Dedication... 3

Ch 1: The Search 4

Ch 2: Mirabelle, The Equation of Balance 12

Ch 3: The Unveiling 22

Ch 4: Who is Michael? 32

Ch 5: The Pharmacy 37

Ch 6: The Hotel 43

Ch 7: Michael and Mirabelle... 49

Ch 8: And Just Like Jack 54

Ch 9: Caleb's Dream, The Cave 57

Ch 10: The Bar.. 60

Ch 11: Why Fred? 73

Ch 12: The Bar Revisited 81

Ch 13: Fred and Caleb.. 91

Ch 14: Tom Phelps 98

Ch 15: Caleb and Mirabelle (Their First Date) 103

Ch 16: Jack Reynolds (Three Months Post the Night with Michael) 113

Ch 17: Tom and Harvey Plus 116

Ch 18: Fred Williams – The Silhouette.................................... 130

Ch 19: A Farewell to Remember 142

Ch 20: Life As We Know It (Two Years Later)........................... 145

Ch 21: A Day on the Set 155

Ch 22: The Premiere of Paperweight 166

Ch 23: The Plight of Heather 178

Ch 24: How We Resolve 186

Ch 25: Curtain Call 191

About the Author 194

ACKNOWLEDGMENTS

This book, a tapestry woven from countless threads of experiences, ideas, and inspirations, would not have seen the light of day without the collective contributions of a remarkable group of individuals and institutions. It is with a heart brimming with gratitude that I extend my sincerest thanks to each one who has journeyed with me through the creation of this work.

To my family, especially my partner, Andria, whose unwavering support, and belief in my vision provided the cornerstone of my motivation and perseverance: your love and patience have been my sanctuary and muse.

I am profoundly grateful to my colleagues and mentors in the field of Information Technology, whose insights and expertise have not only informed much of this work but have also challenged and expanded my own understanding of the digital world. Your willingness to share your knowledge and your encouragement has been invaluable.

My deepest appreciation goes to the brave men and women of the US Army, with whom I had the honor of serving. The lessons learned and the bonds formed during that time have left an indelible mark on my character and on the pages of this book. Your sacrifices and your stories have been a constant source of inspiration and humility.

I must acknowledge the countless authors and storytellers (Faith Gardner, Dean Koontz, John Grisham, Stephen King, Lee Child, Andy Weir, Colleen Hoover, Bonnie Garmus, and Tessa Bailey) who have filled my life with their narratives. Your words have been a refuge and an inspiration, guiding my own storytelling journey.

Special thanks are due to the editorial team and the publishing house for their faith in this project and their meticulous attention to detail. Your professionalism and passion for bringing stories to life have made all the difference.

Finally, to you, the reader, thank you for embarking on this journey with me. It is my hope that within these pages, you find moments of reflection, connection, and a spark of inspiration to pursue your own stories.

This book is a celebration of the collaborative spirit and the collective wisdom that have guided me to this point. To all of you who have been part of this journey, in ways both big and small, thank you from the bottom of my heart.

DEDICATION

To Paxton and Madison, whose laughter and curiosity light up the darkest of rooms and fill my world with endless wonder—this book is a testament to the boundless inspiration you provide me every day.

And to Andria, my rock and my guiding star, whose love and support give me the strength to pursue my dreams and the courage to face any challenge—this journey is ours, together.

With all my love and gratitude,

Stephen McGill

Chapter 1

THE SEARCH

Lakota Junior High School proudly bore the Eagle as its mascot, a symbol steeped in a fable suggesting that an eagle had guided Lewis and Clark throughout their exploratory endeavors. Engraved on the school's walls were snippets of ancient poetry, like "Solace was her name and fear struck cold in the heart," whose meanings were largely lost on the students and faculty alike. These cryptic lines of verse became increasingly obscure deeper within the school's halls, their significance overlooked by the bustling student body.

The school was surrounded by an expansive forest area, discreetly located beyond the lively First Avenue and amidst a sizable, secluded residential neighborhood. Furthermore, the school was a bustling hub for nearly two thousand students, with a considerable portion of them arriving daily from the densely populated city of Federal Way. The city housed people from various backgrounds, which created a diverse student body, as well as racial and economic division. More often than not, the economically advantaged students were distinguished by their lighter skin tones, in stark contrast to their less affluent peers who had darker, more sun-exposed skin.

For Caleb Garcia, a young student at Lakota Junior High, these divisions of social and economic status seemed to blur into insignificance. His interactions with fellow students were so limited that his number of meaningful exchanges could barely fill the fingers of one hand. In his world, the usual boundaries of race and wealth seemed to dissolve, only to be replaced by an aversion to him that cut across all social distinctions.

Despite these challenges, Caleb tried to bridge the gap, making overtures toward inclusion by attempting to join various groups *of students in the lunchroom. His efforts were invariably met with cold rejection. Groups would promptly rise and move to another table upon his approach, leaving him in a palpable state of isolation. This pattern of social ostracization intensified Caleb's feelings of self-doubt, which reached a critical point one spring afternoon, near the end of his eighth-grade year. That day emerged as a pivotal moment in Caleb's life, profoundly influencing his sense of identity and perception of masculinity and paving the way for his future accomplishments. It was a day marked by significant emotional turmoil, yet it also catalyzed a transformative journey, challenging him to navigate and overcome the complex web of social hierarchies and prejudices that characterized his school environment.*

Attending Spanish class became a tri-weekly challenge for Caleb, meticulously scheduled from 10am to 11:20am on Mondays, Wednesdays, and Fridays. The anticipation of these sessions filled him with dread, and he often found himself longing for an extended weekend to avoid his discomfort. Within each of the eighty-minute classes, Caleb engaged in a silent countdown, meticulously tracking all four thousand eight hundred seconds as they slowly ticked by. To pass the time, he would lose himself in the simple pleasures of nature, such as watching a squirrel or a bird through the classroom window, even going so far as to count the bird's feathers, which he consistently estimated to be fourteen.

In an effort to reduce his anxiety (or stress) in the class, Caleb devised a careful exit strategy. When the bell rang, he meticulously timed the submission of his homework and his departure to allow himself to slip through the crowds of students bustling through the hallways. This tactic was born from a need to navigate the social complexities of school life with minimal confrontation. For example, during lunch Caleb would hide in a small classroom that had been abandoned for many years.

Adding to Caleb's struggles was the distinct French accent of Mrs. Flavin, the appointed Spanish teacher. Despite being selected for her bilingual abilities, it became evident the school board had neglected to thoroughly assess her proficiency in Spanish, a language she had only begun to master in recent years. To her credit, Mrs. Flavin did work to improve her Spanish language skills, engaging in nightly study sessions involving listening to Spanish audio tapes and immersing herself in telenovelas. Nevertheless, her persistent French accent tinged her instruction, resulting in a learning environment as unique as it was flawed. Her students, Caleb included, were thus exposed to a version of Spanish distinctly marked by this linguistic idiosyncrasy, complicating their understanding and mastery of the language.

Although Caleb already viewed himself as an outsider, already hated Spanish class, things took a turn for the worst when he mustered the courage to ask a classmate to the Gumdrop Dance. He was not only promptly rejected but dismissed with such cruelty that he was exposed and humiliated before his peers. This rejection was not merely a moment of personal embarrassment; it evolved into a pivotal episode in Caleb's life at school, involving a relentless, boundless campaign of mockery and bullying.

The spectrum of abuse Caleb faced was broad and unyielding, encompassing a barrage of verbal assaults that targeted everything from his physical appearance to his choice of attire, including his characteristic bow tie. The harassment extended beyond words, with Caleb often pelted with erasers and covered in pencil shavings. An already difficult situation was made worse by the unfortunate intervention of a substitute teacher, Mr. Chesterfield, who, unknowingly, amplified Caleb's misery by drawing the entire class's attention to a derogatory note meant for Caleb, thereby fueling the *cycle of ridicule. The note stated, "I hate you."*

Driven to the brink and desperate to reclaim some semblance of respect and peace, Caleb reached a breaking point. In a moment of profound desperation and defiance, he retaliated against the king of the tormentors, using a binder as his instrument of retribution. The impact was so severe that it rendered his bully unconscious and resulted in the loss of several teeth. This act, drastic as it was, served as a watershed moment for Caleb. Despite the consequences he faced, including suspension from school, the incident paradoxically bestowed upon him a period of respite from the bullying. It was this act of standing up for himself that inadvertently brought a new level of respect from his classmates, contributing significantly to the shaping of his character. Not only did the bullying stop but a new experience emerged. Burning hate became envy. This experience, marked by both its violence and its outcome, played a crucial role in fostering Caleb's resilience and determination, teaching him the complex lessons of standing up for oneself and the unforeseen paths through which respect and personal growth can be achieved. After the events of that spring afternoon, he stood a little taller and walked with just a bit more confidence.

Nevertheless, the eighth grade was a tumultuous time, marked by burgeoning questions about the future and personal identity. After the "binder incident," Caleb Garcia found himself unexpectedly thrust into prominence. This newfound visibility revealed itself fully during the annual student government elections, where positions such as President, Vice President, Treasurer, and Secretary were contested. To his surprise, Caleb was nominated. Traditionally, popularity dictated the nominees, but Caleb's unexpected rise to fame made him the exception.

This nomination for a position in the student government represented a monumental transformation in Caleb Garcia's life at school. Transitioning from a state of relative invisibility to becoming notably recognized among his peers, Caleb found himself relishing in his status change and its associated advantages. This experience instilled in him a sense of self-esteem and value markedly absent from his life prior to this period. The event that came to be widely known as the "binder incident" had effectively rebranded him within the school community. Caleb was no longer perceived merely as an ordinary student; he had become emblematic of resilience and defiance, a young individual who had taken a stand against adversity and emerged with his dignity intact. His peers no longer bullied him, and his tormenters fell by the wayside.

When the call came for Caleb to report to the principal's office to discuss the implications of his nomination, a wave of apprehension momentarily overtook his building confidence. Memories of a previous summons to the same office, under circumstances far less promising, clouded his mind. The journey through the school corridors to the principal's office took on a symbolic significance, resembling a precarious walk along the edge of a cliff, with the potential to either solidify his emerging identity or plunge him back into the shadows of anonymity from which he had only recently emerged. Upon his arrival, the sight of several acquaintances from his recent foray into popularity awaited him, further amplifying the sense of nervous anticipation.

The presence of these newfound friends in the principal's office served as a stark reminder of the volatile nature of social standing, especially within the microcosm of a school environment. Each step Caleb took towards that office, each moment leading up to the encounter, was fraught with a complex mix of emotions: fear, excitement, uncertainty, and a burgeoning sense of self-awareness. This pivotal moment was not just about the potential accolades and recognition that might come from his nomination but about confronting the realities of his past actions, the consequences of standing up for oneself, and the continuous journey of personal growth and self-discovery.

Principal Wilson, a veteran educator and military man, awaited them with a presence that commanded respect, despite his internal doubts about his own achievements. With a career spanning over two decades and a family background marked by a stoic dedication to service, Wilson carried himself with an assurance born of discipline and duty. Yet, beneath his decorated exterior, he harbored a secret fear of being perceived as a fraud.

Addressing the students, Wilson embarked on a motivational speech about defining moments and the trajectory of life's journey, drawing on his rich life experiences to inspire them. However, his philosophical musings initially failed to appeal to his young audience. It wasn't until he officially congratulated them on their nominations for student body president that the message's significance became clear. The students' collective excitement at the announcement marked a pivotal moment, not just in their academic careers, but in their personal development and understanding of leadership and recognition.

In the three weeks following Caleb's unexpected nomination, the school corridors transformed into a battleground of campaign fervor. Posters bearing the candidates' promises and aspirations adorned every available space, with Caleb's visage notably less represented than his opponents'. Despite the odds seemingly stacked against him, Caleb devoted himself to perfecting his speech, iterating through ten drafts in his quest for eloquence.

On the day of the final speeches, the school's auditorium was abuzz with anticipation, its seats divided by grade level, each section an attestation of the students' journeys. The seniors, granted proximity to the exit as a nod to their tenure, awaited the proceedings with a mix of enthusiasm and nostalgia.

Caleb's campaign, markedly understated compared to his peers', did little to dampen his resolve. Awaking before dawn, he revisited his speech, a ritual affirming his determination. His family, while supportive, braced for a modest outcome, counseling Caleb on the value of moral victories. Yet this only fueled his resolve, embedding within him a sense of defiance against the prevailing currents of doubt that had shadowed him since the school year's start.

Principal Wilson's arrival to the podium signaled the commencement of the electoral proceedings. His initial address was met with the spirited chant of the school's fight song, a moment of unity that momentarily bridged the competitive divide. Then began the sequence of speeches for the various offices, with the energy in the room fluctuating with the reception of each candidate's address.

As the presidential speeches approached, Caleb felt the weight of the occasion. The speeches of his opponents, Adam Debay and Jaime Grumman, each focusing on their respective platforms, heightened the tension for Caleb. Adam, with his overbite and slouched appearance, shared a lot of issues with the school and its inability to hold a budget in alignment. Jaime, on the other hand, mentioned only sports in his speech, and attempted to rile the audience up by jumping and screaming. As Caleb's turn was announced with a casual introduction by Principal Wilson, Caleb felt his initial trepidation give way to transformative clarity.

Approaching the podium, Caleb was enveloped by the palpable anticipation of his peers. Opting to forego his meticulously prepared notes, he chose instead to speak candidly, connecting with his audience on a profoundly personal level. His speech, a reflection on his journey and aspirations for the school, resonated deeply, transcending the usual platitudes of student elections.

Caleb's message, emphasizing unity, understanding, and collective action, struck a chord with the audience. His vision for a school where every voice mattered, where challenges were met with collaborative solutions, inspired a sense of possibility among his listeners. The auditorium, often a space of division and competition, became a place of shared dreams and ambitions.

As Caleb concluded, the response was initially one of stunned silence, a collective processing of the sincerity and passion with which he had spoken. Then, as if awakening from a reverie, the students erupted into an ovation, a recognition not just of the speech but of the potential for change Caleb represented.

The subsequent announcement of Caleb's landslide victory was more than a personal triumph; it was a mandate for a new direction, an endorsement of his message of inclusivity and progress. His election, by an unprecedented margin, marked not just the start of his tenure as student body president but the beginning of a new chapter for Lakota Junior High School. One where every student, irrespective of their background or social standing, could find their voice and place. Caleb's journey from an overlooked student to a unifying figure was substantiation of the power of authenticity, empathy, and the courage to envision a better future for all.

Chapter 2

MIRABELLE, THE EQUATION OF BALANCE

Mirabelle's journey through high school was an intricate mosaic of experiences ranging from the intellectually exhilarating to the socially challenging. Like the complex mathematical equations, she found so fascinating, her life during these formative years was a delicate balance of variables and constants, each contributing to the larger, multifaceted equation that defined her adolescence.

In the purview of academics, Mirabelle truly shone, her brilliance undimmed by the rigors of her high school curriculum. Mathematics, with its precise logic and elegant solutions, was a source of pure joy for her. She reveled in the challenge of untangling the most complicated problems, her mind dancing through numbers and formulas with the ease of a seasoned mathematician. This passion for math was not confined to the classroom; it extended into her active participation in the Math Olympics, a competition that brought together the brightest young minds to test their mettle against the intricacies of algebra, geometry, and calculus. Mirabelle's role in these competitions was not just as a participant but as a leader, her innovative approach to problem-solving inspiring her team to push beyond their limits, to find beauty in the complexity of numbers.

Her academic prowess was not limited to mathematics alone. Mirabelle also harbored a deep love for language, a love that was beautifully showcased in her participation in the annual spelling bee. Words fascinated her, each one a key to vast and varied meanings, a puzzle of phonetics and etymology waiting to be solved. The spelling bee was more than a mere competition; it was an arena where she could celebrate her love for the written word, engaging in a delicate dance of vowels and consonants that showcased her linguistic dexterity.

However, the spotlight her academic successes cast upon her also brought with it a shadow of unwanted attention from her male peers. This positive and negative attention was a constant distraction, an unwelcome intrusion into her world of numbers and letters. Mirabelle found herself the object of admiration and infatuation, a situation she navigated with a combination of grace and discomfort. She was adept at deflecting conversations from the personal to the platonic, yet the effort required to maintain this delicate balance was taxing. The attention, while sometimes flattering, was often a source of frustration, a reminder of the social complexities that came with visibility.

Amidst these external challenges, Mirabelle faced a more personal trial. Her younger brother, Michael, was struggling to find his own path in the tumultuous world of high school. His difficulties were a stark contrast to Mirabelle's achievements, a divergence that brought her both pain and determination. Michael's struggles were not a reflection of his intelligence but rather of his ability to engage with the school's curriculum and find relevance in its lessons. Mirabelle took it upon herself to be not only his sister but also his mentor, dedicating countless hours to tutoring sessions, offering both academic support and emotional encouragement. Her efforts were evidence of her deep love and commitment to her brother's well-being, even as they drew her attention away from her pursuits.

The balance Mirabelle sought to maintain between her academic ambitions and her personal life was a constant challenge. Her victories in the Math Olympics and the spelling bee were mo-

ments of personal triumph, yet they were tinged with the awareness of her brother's ongoing struggles. These achievements, while sources of pride, also served as reminders of the delicate equilibrium she strived to maintain—a balance between celebrating her successes and supporting Michael through his trials.

Mirabelle's high school years were thus a period of intense growth and learning, marked by a series of contrasts that shaped her into a resilient, compassionate individual. Her story was one of navigating the complexities of adolescence, of finding joy in the intellectual challenges presented by her studies while also confronting the social and personal trials that accompanied her journey. Through it all, Mirabelle remained an example of dedication and love, her life a reflection of the intricate equations she so loved to solve, each variable and constant playing its part in the larger story of her high school years.

Within the structured confines of the classroom, Mirabelle thrived, her affinity for mathematics illuminating her academic path with the brilliance of a guiding star. Her participation in the Math Olympics stood was affirmation of her exceptional abilities, where she not only competed but led her team with a level of expertise and enthusiasm that was truly remarkable. The Math Olympics was not merely a competition; it was a battleground of intellect where the most challenging problems awaited, each a complex labyrinth of numbers and theories. These problems were not solved through rote memorization or simple calculation but required a deep well of creativity and critical thinking for their resolution. Mirabelle's approach to these mathematical puzzles was nothing short of inspirational. With an infectious zeal, she plunged into each problem, her mind dancing through the intricacies of algebraic expressions and geometric configurations, unraveling them with an elegance that seemed almost effortless. Her leadership was pivotal;

under her guidance, her team navigated through the complexities of the competition, finding within themselves capabilities they had not known they possessed. Together, they explored innovative pathways to solutions, their collective success anchored by Mirabelle's unwavering confidence and sharp intellect.

In a different arena, yet parallel in the demand for excellence and love for the subject, was Mirabelle's engagement with the annual spelling bee. Here, her fascination with the world of words showcased another dimension of her academic prowess. For Mirabelle, words were not mere tools of communication but intricate puzzles that held within them layers of meaning and history. Her passion for numbers was matched only by her love for language, a dual affinity that made her a formidable contender in the spelling bee. This event was much more to her than a mere competition; it was a profound celebration of the intricacies and nuances of the English language. Each round of the spelling bee brought with it the thrill of navigating through the phonetic complexities and etymological wonders of words, each one a key to unlock meanings both simple and profound. Mirabelle reveled in the rhythm and flow of syllables, in the delicate dance of consonants and vowels that came together to create words capable of conveying the vast spectrum of human experience. The spelling bee was an arena where she could immerse herself in the beauty of language, demonstrating her understanding and respect for its power to not only define and describe but also to enchant and mislead.

Mirabelle's dual pursuits in mathematics and language arts highlighted her unique academic profile, one that straddled the logical precision of math and the expressive richness of language. Her achievements in both the Math Olympics and the spelling bee were not merely personal victories but celebrations of her multifaceted intellect and her ability to inspire those around her. Through her endeavors, she exemplified the importance of both logic and creativity, showing that the pursuit of knowledge was not confined to a single domain but was an expansive, interconnected journey. Her passion for these disciplines, coupled with her leadership and innovative thinking, not only led her teams to victory but also left a lasting impact on her peers, encouraging them to explore their interests with the same fervor and dedication that she embodied.

Mirabelle's journey through high school, marked by a spectrum of academic accolades and intellectual triumphs, was not without its share of tribulations. Beyond the structured environment of classrooms and the objective assessment of competitions, she encountered a domain of social dynamics that proved to be challenging in a manner entirely distinct from the academic hurdles she so adeptly overcame. The recognition she garnered from her exceptional performance in school competitions, while affirming her intellectual prowess, also cast her into the spotlight of male attention, a spotlight she found both uncomfortable and distracting. This attention, stemming from her achievements, became a double-edged sword. On one hand, it substantiated her hard work and talent, yet, on the other, it invited a level of personal scrutiny and social interaction she found unwelcome.

Navigating this attention required a delicate balance of diplomacy and detachment. Mirabelle endeavored to maintain a polite yet firm distance, channeling conversations away from the personal and back towards the safer, more neutral territories of academic discussions or light-hearted trivialities. Her attempts to redirect these interactions were not just efforts to preserve her comfort but also to maintain her focus on her academic and extracurricular pursuits, areas where she felt her energies were best invested. Despite these efforts, the constant need to manage and deflect this *attention proved to be a significant distraction, one that demanded a portion of her mental and emotional bandwidth, detracting from her studies and her passion projects.*

Compounding these external distractions was a more personal and pressing concern within her own family. Mirabelle's younger brother, Michael, was navigating his own set of challenges, ones that stood in stark contrast to the high-flying academic trajectory of his sister. Michael's struggles in school were not rooted in a lack of intelligence but stemmed from issues of focus, motivation, and, perhaps, the daunting shadow of his sister's accomplishments. This discrepancy between the siblings' academic experiences became a source of concern for Mirabelle, who felt a profound sense of responsibility for her brother's well-being and academic success.

Driven by a deep familial bond and sense of duty, Mirabelle took on the role of Michael's tutor, advocate, and unwavering supporter. Her efforts to assist her brother went beyond mere academic tutoring; she sought to bolster his confidence, reignite his motivation, and help him find his own path to success. This role added another layer of complexity to Mirabelle's already busy life, requiring her to juggle her own academic commitments with the time and emotional energy needed to support Michael. Her dedication to her brother's cause was a testament to her character, showcasing her ability to extend her leadership and compassion beyond the ambits of mathematics and spelling bees and into the more challenging arena of personal adversity.

Mirabelle's navigation of these distractions—the unwelcome attention from her peers and the more pressing concerns surrounding her brother's academic struggles—highlighted her resilience and adaptability. These experiences, though challenging, contributed to her growth as an individual, teaching her valuable lessons in empathy, boundary-setting, and the importance of family. Through it all, Mirabelle remained committed to her academic pursuits, her extracurricular activities, and most importantly, to her role as a supportive sister, demonstrating that her capabilities extended far beyond the confines of classrooms and competition stages.

Her accomplishments in the academic realm, particularly her successes in the Math Olympics and the spelling bee, were sources of immense pride but also carried a tinge of melancholy. Even amidst the accolades and the applause, Mirabelle's thoughts often drifted to Michael, pondering the depths of her contributions to his struggles and questioning whether her efforts were sufficient or if she could do more to uplift him. The sweetness of her victories was thus tempered by a persistent concern for her brother, casting a shadow of bittersweet complexity over her achievements.

This chapter in Mirabelle's life was emblematic of her extraordinary resilience, strength, and unwavering sense of dedication to the people she held dear. It was a period characterized by significant personal growth, as she navigated the treacherous waters of receiving both wanted and unwanted attention, all while striving to meet the demands placed upon her by her exceptional talents and the needs of her family. The challenges she faced forced her to develop a keen sense of empathy and an ability to set boundaries, skills that would serve her well beyond the halls of her high school.

Throughout this tumultuous time, Mirabelle remained a pillar of steadfast determination and compassion. Her story is a compelling tribute to the idea that the most challenging equations in life are not those found in textbooks or competitions but those that involve the human heart. The victories she cherished most were not merely the ones accompanied by trophies and accolades, but those quieter, more personal triumphs achieved in the radius of family and personal growth. Mirabelle's experiences underscored the *profound truth that true success is not always measured by public recognition but often found in the strength to support and uplift those we love, even when doing so requires sacrificing our desires and ambitions.*

Through every trial and triumph, Mirabelle exemplified the essence of true leadership and the depth of familial loyalty, proving that the most enduring victories are those that contribute to the well-being of others. Her journey through high school was not just a series of academic competitions won or challenges faced; it was a deeply personal odyssey of learning to balance the scales of personal ambition with the weight of familial responsibility, a journey marked by the realization that the most significant achievements are often those accomplished in the quiet moments of support and sacrifice for those we hold most dear.

In the years following her graduation from high school, Mirabelle embarked on a path that diverged significantly from the one she had once envisioned for herself. She was on the path of becoming a highly respected and honored mathematician, but with a sense of duty and love that eclipsed her personal ambitions, she dedicated herself to supporting her brother, Michael, in ways that went beyond the conventional expectations of sisterly support. Their parents were emotionally and physically absent, overly invested in their own careers, and did not have the time nor capacity to provide the necessary guidance and support. Mirabelle filled the void they created, acting not just as a sister but as a guardian and mentor. The decision to forgo her academic pursuits, particularly the opportunity to attend college, was monumental. It was a sacrifice born from an unwavering commitment to her brother's future, ensuring that he had the foundation and support needed to complete his high school education—a journey they embarked on together, with Mirabelle taking on the roles of tutor, motivator, and steadfast supporter.

When Michael expressed a desire to move to Los Angeles to become the next big actor, Mirabelle did not hesitate to support him. The decision to move, when Mirabelle was twenty-one and Michael was twenty, meant leaving behind whatever familiarity and security they had. It was a leap of faith—confirmation of Mirabelle's belief in her brother's potential and her dedication to his well-being. Their parents handed them each five hundred dollars and asked that they visit during major holidays.

Los Angeles, with its sprawling landscapes and myriad possibilities, represented a new chapter in their lives: a chance for Michael to pursue his dreams and for Mirabelle to explore a new facet of her own journey of self-discovery and growth.

This move was not just a change of location; it was a bold step into a future filled with unknowns. Mirabelle, in her unwavering support for Michael, demonstrated a remarkable ability to adapt and thrive in the face of change. Together, they navigated the complexities of a new city, with Mirabelle working various jobs to support them while continuing to be Michael's anchor and guide. The challenges they faced in Los Angeles—finding their place in a city known for both its opportunities and its hardships—further solidified their bond and highlighted Mirabelle's resilience and versatility.

Mirabelle worked as a receptionist, an extra in TV shows and movies, and eventually as a bartender. Her skills in next-level mathematics were reserved for counting ounces of liquor and bottles of booze. In a world where resentment is palpable, she had very little. Her love for her brother superseded any life goals that she had.

In return, her brother, Michael, felt a freedom that was not lost on him. He recognized that without Mirabelle's unconditional love *he would have a much different life. A life of disconnection from the human condition. In a parallel world, Mirabelle would have been a professor of advanced calculus, and Michael would have lived with his parents, unable to have any meaningful relationships.*

Through it all, Mirabelle's story evolved into a powerful narrative of loyalty, sacrifice, and the profound impact of putting someone else's needs and dreams ahead of one's own. Her decision to support Michael at the cost of her own ambitions was a choice that redefined her sense of purpose and success. In the end, Mirabelle's journey with Michael through the trials and triumphs of post-high school life and their venture into the vastness of Los Angeles was a profound demonstration of the enduring nature of sibling bonds and the immeasurable value of selfless love and support.

Chapter 3

THE UNVEILING

The blazing sun illuminated the chaos outside a sizable, unadorned structure. This building, clinical and plain, cloaked in an unexceptional hue of brown, stood in sharp contrast to the vivid neon signage reading On the Set, which was a seemingly a flame of creativity in an otherwise mundane setting. Amidst the flurry of production staff and the constant movement of equipment was Caleb Garcia. Now in his early thirties, Caleb's outward youthful vigor masked the deep reservoirs of experience and the myriad challenges he had navigated in his life. Surrounded by cameras that ceaselessly captured every nuance of his presence—from the perspiration glistening on his brow to the slight, involuntary quivers of apprehension—he found himself struggling to light a cigarette.

The unexpected arrival of a limousine cut through the tension, its sleek form gliding into view like a promise of temporary sanctuary. Seizing the opportunity, Caleb made a swift move toward the vehicle, opened its side door, and slid in. He left behind the curious stares and humming energy of the crew, who, in turn, migrated back toward building's shelter.

This momentary withdrawal into the limousine wasn't merely an escape from the physical environment but a symbolic retreat from the pressures of being constantly observed and judged. Inside the vehicle, Caleb found a fleeting sense of privacy and reflection, a chance to shed the role he was playing and confront the complexities of his own identity. The contrast between the bustling activity outside and the quietude within the limousine highlighted the duality of Caleb's existence: his public persona and the introspective individual seeking moments of solitude amidst the chaos *of life in the spotlight.*

Inside the limousine's opulent interior, the air was thick with the tension as it stood in total contrast of the months Caleb had spent in rehab/on On the Set. Tom Phelps, Caleb's agent, personified Hollywood's seasoned veneer—his artificially tanned skin and impeccably white teeth clashed with the sincerity of the moment. Overweight and forthright, Tom's demeanor hinted at a man who had navigated too many crises, his direct tone masking an underlying fear of failure.

Tom broke the silence, his voice cutting through the hum of the engine. "I got your pages from the center, and I have the publisher set for a July release."

Caleb leaned forward; his interest piqued despite the weariness lining his face. "What about the advance?" he asked, hope threading through his words.

Tom's response came with a hesitant pause. "I could only pull twenty grand from them."

"Twenty?" Caleb's voice cracked slightly, a mixture of disbelief and desperation. "What about the movie option you told me about?"

"That is a whole other bowl of wax," Tom said, his attempt at levity falling flat in the charged atmosphere.

Caleb frowned; confusion etched across his brow. "What is a bowl of wax?"

"I think you get what I'm saying," Tom replied, evasively.

"No, really," Caleb pressed, unwilling to let the matter drop.

Tom sighed; the sound heavy with the weariness of countless negotiations. "I have published six of your novels, and we have optioned three screenplays. You should understand by now that you get no money upfront, but you get one percent of the back end."

The words hung between them, a stark reminder of the realities of their world. "That ended up being ten thousand dollars last time," Caleb pointed out, the sting of past disappointments palpable in his voice.

"You know this is a good deal. And Manchild was a terrible movie, terrible concept, honestly it was just terrible. Truth be told, we should have paid them to make it," Tom retorted, his attempt at humor doing little to lighten the mood.

"I just can't be broke," Caleb said.

"Well, I am not your accountant, and you just went to a rehab that cost ten grand a week, so you might want to figure out your next move fast."

"You are my agent, and this was all your idea."

Tom leaned back, his expression softening slightly. "Oh, come on, it was best for you at the time. I mean, you were really going off the deep end there, and plus, you got to be on the show, and it's supposed to be great. It's like your own launch vehicle."

Caleb's anger broke through the veneer of calm. "I didn't want my own launch vehicle," he spat, the words laced with bitterness. "I wanted my life back, and now everyone is going to see me going through my own personal hell on television."

"You did it to yourself," Tom replied, his voice devoid of sympathy.

"Did what?" Caleb's confusion was palpable.

"Put yourself in a position of need," Tom explained, as if speaking to a child.

24

Caleb shook his head, frustration mounting. "I don't think you understand the total concept here. I have genius in me still. You think, since I went to rehab and quit drugs and alcohol, that the gift is gone? Oh, the gift is not gone. In fact, the gift is about to rear its ugly head."

The limousine turned a corner, the movement highlighting the chasm that had formed between the two men—between the artist who fought to retain his essence and the agent who navigated the treacherous waters of commercial success. The conversation, a dance of frustration and misunderstanding, continued to unfold, a corroboration of the complex interplay of creativity, ambition, and the harsh realities of a life lived in the public eye.

"Maybe you lost your magic touch even before you went to rehab," Tom remarked, his voice laced with a thinly veiled sarcasm that did little to mask his underlying concern.

"It's not like graduate school. It is not like you can go again and again and again."

"If people planned it correctly, maybe it could be."

"How would they plan it right?"

"Oh, the gift is not gone, in fact, the gift is about to rear its ugly head."

"I don't feel a sense of loss," Caleb insisted, his denial thick with the pain of recent memories.

"Oh, I think you do. Deep inside, you are feeling alone and lost."

"Maybe alone, but not lost."

"Oh man, are you lost. You don't even know who you are anymore. I read those letters you wrote, man...Lost," Tom remarked, his tone embodying a mix of concern and bewilderment as he touched upon the raw, unvarnished truths that Caleb had laid bare during

rehab. The letters, a collection of Caleb's deepest fears, hopes, and insecurities, offered a glimpse into his soul, revealing the depth of his struggles with identity and purpose.

"Those letters were the desperate cry from an inner child. Your inner child was saying 'I'm lost.'" This was not merely an observation but a diagnosis, an attempt to peel back the layers of Caleb's guarded exterior and expose the vulnerable core that lay beneath. Tom's perspective suggested that the letters were more than just expressions of momentary despair; they were the manifestations of a deeper, unresolved conflict within Caleb, a cry for help from the most innocent and unguarded part of his being.

"You have no idea what you're talking about," Caleb retorted, his response laced with a mixture of indignation and defensiveness. Caleb's patience, already worn thin by the conversation, began to unravel, fraying at the edges.

The exchange between Tom and Caleb was a complex dance of communication and miscommunication, a delicate negotiation between the need to be understood and the fear of being exposed. Tom's intentions, though arguably rooted in a desire to connect with and help Caleb, were met with resistance, a natural response to what Caleb perceived as an attempt to pigeonhole his experiences and feelings.

"I know you lost yourself in that place," Tom persisted, his belief unshaken by Caleb's denial.

"Like it was my choice. You told me it was smart, that the public would love me for it. You actually said that it was a good business move. Are you taking that back now?" Caleb's anger boiled over, the betrayal he felt casting a shadow over their relationship.

"I admit that the publicity we're getting from this is great, but the whole idea that you're bitching about this is just completely prosaic."

"You're using the word prosaic now?" Caleb's disbelief was evident, his voice dripping with scorn.

"It means..." Tom began, but Caleb cut him off.

"I know what it means. I am a writer; it is my job to know what the word prosaic means. Prosaic: to be matter of fact or unimaginative."

"Did you just look up words in the dictionary while you were in rehab?" Tom's attempt at humor missed its mark, further aggravating the rift between them.

"Are you trying to upset me?"

"Are you done yet?" Tom asked, his patience wearing thin.

"Done with what?"

"Arguing with me. I am trying to fix your terrible career here, and you are trying to pick a fight."

"What do you mean, am I done yet? I gave up everything for this."

"You are acting a little like a wounded child right now. Are you five years old, man? Is that you, man? Do you need to be spanked like a child?"

"You're an asshole."

"I can accept that if you can accept the fact that I got you a meeting with the president of Mangold Films,"

"They made Manchild,"

"So, they made some mistakes. But even so, you wrote the script for it. For some reason, they have a thing for you and your one percent of the back end."

"How about I get the money upfront? I'm just tired of going through the motions with this." Caleb's voice was a mixture of weariness, a barely concealed plea for some semblance of control over the direction his life was taking. This request was not just a negotiation tactic; it was an admission of his exhaustion with the unpredictability that had come to define his existence.

"And that is exactly why I got you the meeting. They have hinted at the fact that they might want you on the set, which means a set fee as the writer," Tom remarked, his voice imbued with a confidence that seemed designed to reassure Caleb. In Tom's words lay the promise of a lifeline, an opportunity for Caleb to reclaim some of the acclaim and financial security that had eluded him. This meeting, and the potential it represented, was Tom's gambit, a carefully orchestrated move in the complex chess game of Hollywood deal-making.

This conversation was more than just a negotiation over terms and conditions; it was a pivotal moment in Caleb's life. The possibility of securing an upfront payment and the chance to be directly involved in the adaptation of his work were glimmers of hope in the murky waters of his career. Yet, beneath the surface of this dialogue lay the complexities of their relationship—a blend of professional dependency, mutual respect, and the unspoken tensions that arise when personal struggles collide with artistic integrity and commercial imperatives.

As the limousine continued its journey, it encapsulated the paradox of Caleb's situation—enveloped in luxury yet grappling with turmoil, seated beside a man who represented both his greatest hopes for recovery and the stark realities of an industry known for its ruthlessness. This moment was a microcosm of the broader struggles faced by creative souls in their quest for artistic expression and recognition, underscored by the harsh truths of survival in an *industry that values profit as much as, if not more than, artistry.*

"How much is the set fee?"

"Remember the days when you didn't ask 'how much money?' You just counted it as your bank account swelled over millions of dollars," Tom reminisced, a wistful note in his voice.

"That was before cocaine."

"Oh, the days before cocaine," Tom mused, lost in thought for a moment before Caleb cut in.

"Don't do that."

"What?" Tom looked at him, feigning innocence.

"Make me think about when I used."

"You got to think about something, sometime, someplace. So you used for a while, who cares?" Tom shrugged.

"I care. I wanted to be the best writer I could be, and I ruined it with drugs."

"Drugs and whores. Don't forget the whores."

"I never did anything with whores."

"Oh, yes, that was me," Tom conceded with a chuckle, then his expression sobered. "Well, about that…"

"About what?"

"Kendra might have left," Tom said, his voice dropping.

"What?"

"Kendra left and filed for divorce."

"She really left?" Caleb's voice was barely a whisper, a mix of disbelief and sorrow.

"And filed for divorce."

"How come you didn't tell me until now?"

"You were in rehab, and I didn't want to mess with your deal here. You were writing away on some yellow notepad, and here I was having to hire someone to transcribe your chicken scratch. Yet, somehow, I'm the bad guy."

"When did she leave?"

"Remember the day I dropped you off at rehab?" Tom paused, letting the moment hang between them. "She left the minute you checked in."

"She just said she needed space."

"She did need space, away from you." Tom paused, looked at Caleb, then continued. "Here is what we are going to do; we are going to roll with this problem and come to a solution. This is not the end of the world. This is not that big of a deal. People get divorced, and it is no big deal. This is Hollywood, the home of the rich and famous. Unfortunately for you, you are neither rich nor famous. I mean, you were rich until the drug problem, and you were famous until...your drug problem. You know, I still don't get why some people in this town get a pass, but you, you end up destitute. Did I use that word correctly?"

"Yes," Caleb replied curtly, his mind reeling from the onslaught of revelations.

"You end up in a ditch outside of my house, calling me a loser for not taking that sitcom punch-up job. Do you know who does those kinds of jobs? People who are just starting out...and hacks. I was not about to soil your image," Tom continued, trying to steer the conversation back to the matter at hand.

A long moment of silence passed, the weight of their conversation settling heavily in the air.

"When is this meeting?" Caleb finally asked, resigned to the fact that his life was now in uncharted territory.

Tom opened the limousine door, signaling that they had arrived at their destination. "Right now," he said, a note of finality in his voice.

Caleb looked at Tom with disappointed eyes, a man stripped of his illusions, confronting the harsh realities of his choices. As he stepped out of the limousine and into the glaring sunlight, Caleb Garcia was no longer the celebrated author he once was. He was a man on the brink, searching for redemption in the unforgiving landscape of Hollywood.

Chapter 4

WHO IS MICHAEL?

Outside, the apartment complex loomed under the cover of night, its façade marred by graffiti, evidence of the rough edges of the neighborhood. Under the dim light of the streetlamp, two figures, homeless and lost to desperation, sought solace in each other's company, their bond a stark contrast to the isolation of the streets.

Inside, the world was markedly different, albeit suffused with its own brand of despair. The camera found Michael Tabor, a young man in his mid-twenties, whose slight tan did little to mask the weariness etched into his features. His apartment, a cramped space filled with the aspirations of a man clinging to dreams, was adorned with posters of Jack Reynolds films, each image a symbol of the success for which Michael yearned.

In the quiet solitude of his room, Michael stood before the mirror, engaging in a moment of introspection that briefly allowed a smile to trace his lips. This fleeting expression of confidence, however, was quickly eclipsed by a realization that was trivial in nature yet significant in symbolism. The mismatched color of his shoes, one brown and one black, became an unexpected focal point of his morning ritual. It was a minor detail, yet in Michael's mind, it represented a deviation from the norm, a misalignment between his current circumstances and the aspirations he harbored. With a sense of resigned determination, he reached for a magic marker, embarking on a makeshift endeavor to color his boot black. As he meticulously darkened his shoe, he whispered a mantra of hope to his reflection, "Today you will get the girl because winners get the girl." The words, though softly spoken, resounded with the power of his convictions, imbuing him with a sense of purpose and optimism.

The ritual of self-empowerment continued as Michael listened to affirmations from a tape recorder, a sequence of motivational statements designed to fortify his spirit against the day's uncertainties. This personal pep talk served as a crucial element of his morning routine, a psychological armor against the doubts and fears that threatened his resolve. Each affirmation, played back in his own voice, was a reminder of the strength he possessed within, a call to harness his inner resources and face the world with courage and determination.

As the affirmations echoed in the room, Michael's attention shifted to his digital camera, a repository of recent memories and a visual exhibit of his fascination with Kelly. The small screen of the camera came alive with images of Kelly, each photograph capturing the essence of her beauty and grace. Tall, blonde, and seemingly the epitome of Hollywood's idealized vision of attractiveness, Kelly represented more than just an object of Michael's affection; she was the embodiment of the aspirations that fueled his daily rituals. The photographs, taken with a mix of admiration and longing, were snapshots of a moment in time, a day when Michael had felt close enough to his dream to capture it through his lens.

Kelly's presence in these images, though confined to the digital pixels of a camera screen, loomed large in Michael's psyche. She was at once a symbol of his deepest desires and a reminder of the distance he felt from achieving them.

Compelled by a mixture of longing and desperation, Michael reached for his phone, dialing Kelly's number under the pretense of a lost ID—a maneuver orchestrated the night before when he pocketed her identification. "Hello, Kelly. This is Michael Tabor from the bar. You were there last night, and I noticed that you left your ID," he began, his voice a mixture of hope and calculated calm.

The revelation that Kelly's boyfriend would retrieve the ID, a sharp deviation from Michael's envisioned scenario, played out in a brief exchange. The call, laden with disappointment, ended with Michael's feigned understanding, "Yeah, it happens all the time."

The weight of his failed attempt at connection was palpable as Michael, now visibly crushed, embarked on a symbolic cleansing. He methodically deleted the photographs of Kelly from his camera, each image erased a step-in distancing himself from his unrequited obsession. With a decisive motion, he cut Kelly's ID in half, discarding it in the trash—a gesture of relinquishment.

The silence of the room was broken by the stirrings of the unnamed woman in his bed, her presence a stark reminder of the night's earlier diversions. "What are you doing?" she asked, her voice tinged with confusion and the remnants of sleep.

Michael's response, cold and devoid of the earlier warmth he had reserved for Kelly, marked a stark contrast. "How about you stop worrying about what I am doing and start thinking about leaving?"

"What did you say?" the woman asked, her voice rising in a mix of surprise and indignation.

"You heard me," Michael replied, his tone final.

Tension simmered in the unlit apartment. The unnamed woman confronted him. "Didn't you tell me that you had my ID with you? You never gave it back to me last night," she accused, her voice laced with irritation.

Michael offered a feeble excuse, "I must have lost it." His response did little to quell the growing storm.

"What? You are such an asshole," she retorted.

In a moment of introspection, Michael retrieved the recording device from his pocket, replaying the same affirmation from before: "Today you will get the girl because winners get the girl."

The tape, once a source of motivation, now echoed hollowly in the cramped room. With a decisive motion, he erased the tape, symbolically shedding the persona he had adopted.

As the camera pulled back, revealing the nightstand cluttered with ID cards of ten to fifteen girls, the extent of Michael's charade became apparent. Each card, a trophy from his encounters, stood as a revelation of the façade he maintained. Picking up another ID, Michael's tone shifted, a mixture of resignation and curiosity coloring his voice. "I guess I will just have to move on to...Tiffani, with an 'I'. Oh, how cute is that?"

Suddenly, the atmosphere of the room changed as the director's voice cut through the tension. "And cut...That was great," he announced, stepping out from behind the camera to approach Michael.

"I'm telling you, if we ever get a distributor, we are going to make bundles of money," the director said, his enthusiasm for the project evident despite the looming financial uncertainties.

"But until then, no one gets paid, huh?" Michael replied.

"I want to pay you, but the producers tell me otherwise. I love what you're working with, though. The looks you gave us were incredible," the director tried to reassure him, his praise genuine.

At that moment, Harvey Lewis, Michael's agent, approached, his sharp suit marking him as someone who took his role seriously. "Michael, you were great."

"You really think so?" Michael asked.

"I wouldn't lie to you, man," Harvey affirmed, his confidence in Michael's talent unwavering.

"I'm getting really tired of doing independent movies for no money," Michael confessed, voicing the frustration felt by many *actors in his position.*

"Listen, I got some stuff lined up," Harvey began, his hesitation hinting at the familiar predicament they faced.

"What kind of stuff?" Michael inquired, hope and skepticism intermingling in his voice.

"Ok, well, it is another independent movie for no money, but you are getting your name out there, man. That is the game: get your name out," Harvey explained.

Looking for a semblance of recognition, Michael turned to the director, "Hey Sal, do you know my name?"

The director, puzzled by the question, hesitated before answering, "It's John, right?"

The disconnect between Michael's real identity and the director's perception underscored the reality many actors face in the industry—despite their contributions and the intimacy of working on a project together, they often remain just another name, easily forgotten. This moment of misrecognition served as a poignant reminder of the challenges and anonymity that come with trying to make it in the world of independent cinema.

Chapter 5

THE PHARMACY

Outside the large "Rite Aid" type pharmacy, the day was bustling with activity. Groups of people moved in and out of the building, most leaving with small bags in their hands, their faces brightening at the prospect of relief. The pharmacy, a refuge for those in need, was on the verge of closing for the day.

Inside, the atmosphere was charged with the tension of the impending closure. Heather Anderson, a thin blonde woman, stood anxiously in line, clutching three prescriptions in her hands. Her attire was representative of a high-ranking executive, though it looked worn, aged. Her frustration was palpable as she glanced between the prescriptions and the clock, which ominously read 4:58pm. The sign above the counter left no room for interpretation: "Pharmacy closes at 5pm, no exceptions."

Impatient and desperate, Heather addressed the person in front of her, her voice tinged with urgency. "Do you need your prescription filled today? Or can you wait?" The response was a cold shoulder. Heather's frustration grew; her brow furrowed in annoyance as the clock ticked closer to the hour.

Finally, as the clock struck 5:00, Heather approached the counter, only to be met with the disapproving gaze of the pharmacist. William, balding and evidently weary from the day's work, glanced at his watch with a look of disgust.

"Hi, I have three prescriptions that need to be filled, and I do realize that I am here just a smidge too late, but I need to have these filled tonight."

"I will need to see if I can even..." William began, his voice trailing off as he examined the prescriptions.

"Even what?"

"This prescription is very old. I can't just fill prescriptions because people want me to. There is a procedure. I have a boss who checks on me, and I could get fired," William explained.

"Look at me. Do I look like someone who cares?" Heather retorted, her frustration reaching a boiling point.

"You're just shooting sunshine up my ass now, aren't you?"

"You don't get it," Heather insisted.

"No, I get it. You're trying to score, and I'm supposed to be the one who tells you 'No.'"

"No, you don't understand. I need these filled right now."

As William scrutinized the prescriptions, his skepticism was evident. "I can only assume that you are not George Anderson."

"Okay, you see, I can explain that. George Anderson is my grandfather, and I am here to pick up his medication for him," Heather said, hoping to clarify the misunderstanding.

"Your grandfather, huh?" William replied.

"Exactly," Heather affirmed, her gaze imploring him to understand the gravity of her request.

In the sterile environment of the pharmacy, the standoff between Heather Anderson and William, the pharmacist, escalated quickly from a simple request to a complex moral and legal debate.

"I don't believe you for a second, but I am obligated to check the validity of the prescription."

"Check away. I am more than happy to wait. And when you find out it is completely legal, I will be looking for you to apologize to me."

"Apologize for what? Doing my job?"

"The Nazis were just doing their jobs,"

"You see the sign out there? It says Bill's Drug Store, not 'Gestapo.'"

"Can you just do your job and fill the prescription?" Heather demanded.

"Let me go see if I can take care of this for you."

As William conferred with another staff member, pointing toward Heather, and discussing the situation, she became visibly nervous and confused. The moment he turned to enter data into the computer, Heather, in a sudden panic, knocked over a sunscreen display and bolted toward the exit, only to be blocked by a large security guard.

Soon thereafter, Heather found herself ensnared in a tense predicament in the back office, sharing the limited space with William and a stoic security guard. The stark reality of her situation began to crystallize, enveloping her in a mix of fear and disbelief. The office, cluttered with files and surveillance equipment, felt increasingly like a cell as the gravity of the accusation against her took hold.

"I just want you to know that we have called the authorities, and you will be prosecuted."

"I didn't do anything," Heather countered, her voice laced with a desperation that betrayed her attempts at maintaining composure.

"George Anderson has been dead for three years, and for some reason, you have continued to refill his pain pill prescriptions," William disclosed.

"But what? You have no idea what is going on here. You think that you know but you have no idea," Heather shot back.

"Well, it's not my place to know; it is my place to find out where the problem is and call the authorities," William retorted, his stance unyielding. His duty, as he saw it, was to protect the integrity of the store and uphold the law, even if it meant ensnaring someone in a legal battle that could alter the course of their life.

Heather's retort was laced with sarcasm and desperation. "Confident, huh? Do you think I am teaching a fucking Tony Robbins seminar over here? I am trying to acquire prescription pills. Do you think I like doing this?"

Her tirade continued, mocking William's name and the situation with biting humor. "Oh, Bill is a better name than William. William sounds really official. William is a single guy's name. A single guy with no prospects, whereas Bill is a man of mystery who is STD-free. William has the clap; Bill, no clap..."

"You sure have a smart mouth for someone who is in big trouble," William observed, unamused by her attempt to lighten the gravity of her predicament.

"Am I, William? Am I in big trouble, or am I just an innocent bystander to the system? The system that named you William instead of Bill."

"I am just a pharmacist who is doing his job. Protecting your health."

"Okay, here's the problem. Here's the real issue. I am an addict, and you have pills, so, my grandfather by the way, who is George Anderson, deceased or not deceased, would have wanted me to be happy and for you to give me his pills. Now you're messing with the spirit of a man who wants to make me happy."

"I am sure that he would have loved for you to take his pills."

"How would you know what he would have loved? You didn't even know him, and furthermore, he would not have liked you at all either because he was a man of honor and integrity—oh, oh, and manners. You haven't even offered me a glass of water or a tic-tac. What am I supposed to think of you, that you are some good guy? So far all you have shown me is that you can take a nice lady, like me, and put me in some sort of holding center."

"This is hardly a holding center," William explained, attempting to steer the conversation back to the matter at hand. "It is the system, not me. The system protects people, people who decide to break the law."

"What does hardly mean? I mean it either is or isn't. I believe my grandpa George would be very disappointed in the way you're treating me right now. I mean, at least a cup of water. How hard is that to do, man? Bring me a drink already. I am parched over here," Heather demanded, her request bordering on the theatrical.

William, perhaps out of a desire to de-escalate the situation or simply to fulfill a basic human courtesy, acquiesced. "I guess that isn't a huge request. I will get you a bottled water," he said, exiting the room momentarily.

Left alone with the security guard, Heather's attention shifted. "What is your name? Mr. Security Guard?" she inquired, seeking to engage him in her web of dialogue.

"I don't have a name. I have a job, and my job is to tell you to shut your mouth," the guard responded, his patience wearing thin.

"You might be a William as well...Oh, William...William, William. William really is a terrible name. You could have been named Edward or Nate, but William?" Heather mused, turning her attention to a magazine as William came back with the water.

After a brief pause and a sip, Heather, seemingly unfazed by the gravity of her situation, quipped, "Have you ever thought of changing your name to Kendal?"

Chapter 6

THE HOTEL

In the plush lounge of a high-end hotel, Tom and Caleb found themselves ensconced on a couch that offered more comfort than Caleb seemed capable of absorbing. Tom wore a black suit, and Caleb wore a traditional business casual attire. The lounge, with its sophisticated bar manned by Mirabelle and Michael in crisp hotel uniforms, exuded an air of casual luxury. Yet, despite the inviting ambiance, Caleb's leg bounced with a nervous energy that seemed at odds with the setting.

"Could you stop doing that?"

"What?"

"You're shaking your leg like you're being interrogated."

"Tom, I just got out of rehab."

"And you're trying to get your career back in order. Don't mess it up by making her think you're coming out of an insane asylum," Tom advised, his words sharp but not without concern.

"Would that be better for my career?"

"Probably."

In response, Caleb ceased the shaking of his leg, only to stand and begin nervously chewing on his nails, a substitution of one anxious habit for another.

"Is this better?"

"If you're auditioning for Chainsaw Massacre, then it's perfect."

"What do you want me to do? I have all this nervous energy

and nowhere to expend it."

"Just sit down and relax. You know what? Let me get you a drink."

Caleb resettled into his seat, a mix of resignation and anxiety in his posture. "I can't drink. That is a gateway," he stated firmly, a reminder of the delicate balance he was trying to maintain in his recovery.

"Caleb, it is only a gateway if you let it be." Tom gestured casually towards the bar, signaling his intent to order drinks, an attempt to ease the tension that Caleb wore like a second skin.

As Mirabelle, the bar manager, approached with an air of professionalism mixed with warmth, she introduced herself and inquired about their drink preferences. Tom, ever the instigator, ordered a vodka for himself and scotch on the rocks for Caleb.

Mirabelle's interaction with Caleb was light, yet it underscored the surreal turn his day had taken—from the structured environment of rehab to the unpredictable social landscape of a hotel bar. As she promised to return with their drinks, Tom, in a gesture of celebration or perhaps defiance, invited her to join them in a toast to Caleb's new beginning, a concept Caleb himself seemed to grapple with.

Once Mirabelle had departed, Tom's attention shifted to what he perceived as an opportunity for Caleb, oblivious or perhaps indifferent to the emotional turmoil his friend was experiencing. "So, what do you think?" Tom pressed, eager to distract or redirect Caleb's focus.

Caleb's response was tinged with disbelief and a hint of resignation. "Not sure what to think. Three hours ago, I was in a rehabilitation facility, and now I'm in a bar. It seems kind of counterproductive."

But Tom was undeterred, steering the conversation towards Mirabelle and the potential he saw for Caleb, regardless of the latter's recent discovery of his wife's departure.

"Tom, you have got to be kidding. I just found out my wife left me, three hours ago!"

"But you have been single for three months. You just didn't know it. Thus, an opportunity. You should ask her out."

Caleb's frustration with Tom's lack of empathy was evident. "You have no regard for other people, do you?" he challenged, his voice a mixture of disbelief and anger.

"I have high regard for others, as long as they are contributing, either directly or indirectly, to my client's well-being," Tom replied.

As Caleb pondered his circumstances, the absurdity of his current predicament struck him. "What am I doing here?"

In the cozy ambiance of the hotel lounge, Tom attempted to bolster Caleb's spirits amidst the latter's evident anxiety. "You are here to jump-start your career and take the next step in your life," Tom affirmed, his voice cutting through the silence that had settled between them. Caleb, unable to fully contain his nervous energy, resumed the leg-tapping that had earlier drawn Tom's mild rebuke. The momentary pause that followed was broken only by the return of Mirabelle, who gracefully delivered their drinks.

As Tom initiated a toast, he unwittingly spotlit Caleb, referring to him by his full name and attracting Mirabelle's attention. "Wait, Caleb Garcia?" she interjected, her interest piqued. Caleb's modest reply, "I used to be," only added to the intrigue, prompting further inquiry from Mirabelle.

The conversation that unfolded revealed Mirabelle's admiration for Caleb's work, particularly his book Manchild, which she confessed had been a favorite during her college years. This unexpected praise seemed to momentarily lift Caleb's spirits, even as Tom playfully chided the film adaptation. Mirabelle's respect for Caleb's craft was evident as she expressed her awe, noting the disparity often found between the persona of creatives and the depth of their creativity.

The exchange culminated in Mirabelle expressing a desire to meet Caleb over coffee, curious about his creative process—a proposition that was somewhat derailed by Tom's eagerness to complete his toast. Nevertheless, the moment served as a poignant reminder of Caleb's impact through his writing.

As the trio raised their glasses to celebrate Caleb's talents, the gesture marked a brief respite from Caleb's tumultuous journey, a reminder of the enduring legacy of his work. And as Mirabelle returned to her duties behind the bar, Tom seized the moment to reassure Caleb, "You, see? People still like you."

As Tom and Caleb continued to await their guest, the air buzzed with tension and anticipation. Caleb's impatience was palpable, his concern for his dwindling career evident in his voice. "Is he ever going to get here? I mean, I do have a life I'm trying to pull back together," *he expressed, a hint of desperation creeping into his tone.*

Tom, ever pragmatic, responded with a mixture of reality and reassurance. "A, you don't really have a life to pull back together. And B, he is a she, she is the best bet we have, and I think you might want to take this a little more seriously."

Before Caleb could dive deeper into his frustrations, Heather Anderson made her entrance. Her confident stride and keen presence immediately shifted the atmosphere. As introductions were made and the trio settled into their seats, it became clear that Heather and Caleb shared a history that extended beyond professional boundaries and into shared struggles.

Caleb immediately noticed in Heather parts of himself. Only later did he connect the dots around addiction.

"We have met before, right?" Caleb inquired, trying to place Heather within the context of his past.

"I am the president of Mangold Films," Heather confirmed, her identity igniting a spark of recognition in Caleb.

The conversation that followed uncovered layers of past interactions and shared experiences between Heather and Caleb, dating back to a time before Caleb's rise as a celebrated author and Heather's venture into film production. Heather reminisced about an audition from 1994, revealing a spontaneous moment of passion between her and Caleb that seemed to surprise even them.

As Heather recounted their unexpected kiss during the audition, Michael approached the table, his attention caught by the unlit cigarette in Heather's hand. His polite reminder about the no-smoking policy prompted a playful yet pointed rebuke from her.

"Can you not see that I am in the middle of a story? I am telling my friend here, Tom, that Caleb and I, you know, Caleb Garcia, the famous author, and Tom..." Heather trailed off, her annoyance evident. The interruption led to a light-hearted exchange about Tom's last name, which Heather feigned forgetting.

"It's not even lit! But, if you want to take away from me the one joy I have in life, then go on and take it," she protested. The situation escalated comically as Heather challenged Michael to take the unlit cigarette from her hand, a task he completed with visible reluctance and embarrassment before quickly retreating.

Caleb stared at a packet of sugar and daydreamed. Heather's response, "At least it is not the real stuff," hinted at a blend of humor and understanding, recognizing Caleb's struggle with addiction and his unconventional method of coping. Caleb's admission, "I am an addict and difficult situations make me tense," revealed the depth of his turmoil, his actions a cry for some semblance of control or relief.

The conversation took a turn toward the absurd as Tom, Heather, and Caleb expounded the comparative merits of snorting cocaine versus sugar.

Heather, ever the pragmatist amidst the unfolding chaos, shared her journey from recreational drug use to a more socially acceptable dependency on prescription medications, rationalizing her choices with a logic that seemed to fit the peculiar tone of their discussion. Tom could only label the situation as "awful," a sentiment underscored by Caleb's continued pantomime of drug use with sugar, an act of defiance against his struggles.

As Heather attempted to steer the conversation back to her earlier anecdote involving a passionate moment shared with Caleb during an audition, the narrative momentarily shifted from the complexities of addiction to a simpler time when their biggest concern was the chemistry between them. This fleeting memory of youthful indiscretion and ambition was punctuated by a shared exclamation of "TADA" after a director's cut, a light-hearted end to a moment of intense connection.

Chapter 7

MICHAEL AND MIRABELLE

Mirabelle took her break at a corner table of the bar, sipping her coffee, her eyes scanning the room filled with people. Her brother, Michael, joined her, wearing a mischievous grin on his face.

"Did you know that Caleb Garcia is sitting over there?"

"Who is Caleb Garcia?"

"Remember that movie Manchild?"

"I love that movie."

"Well, he wrote the book."

Mirabelle arched an eyebrow, "I don't really read books."

"But you do understand that before a film is made, the words are written down on paper, and sometimes the stories are taken from books."

"Of course. Everyone knows that," Mirabelle replied, slightly amused. "My apologies, from your comment before, I figured I was speaking to a seven-year-old."

Michael chuckled, "I am only seven on the inside. I am all man on the outside."

"I don't know why I let you speak to me like that."

"If we weren't related, you would probably not let me."

"That's it; you are officially not my brother."

"It is difficult to hear my awesome thoughts when you are always talking."

"Awesome thoughts? Yesterday you told me that you had an audition for a cat commercial, but all you did was watch a marathon of Real Housewives.".

"That is a great show."

Mirabelle's question cut through the air, a mixture of curiosity and concern evident in her tone, "What happened to the audition?" She was genuinely interested in her brother's pursuits, despite her reservations about his choices.

Michael, with a hint of resignation in his voice, responded, "My manager called and told me that they were recasting it with all females." His words carried a mix of disappointment and acceptance, a reflection of the unpredictable nature of the industry he was trying to break into.

Mirabelle, seeking clarification and perhaps a bit of levity in the situation, couldn't help but point out, "You mean our neighbor, Ted" emphasizing the informal and perhaps unconventional nature of Michael's representation.

With a nod, Michael acknowledged her point but quickly defended his choice, "Don't get mad at me because Bill is my manager."

Mirabelle, unable to contain her skepticism, rolled her eyes and retorted, "Bill is an unemployed trust fund baby."

"Michael, you've been at this for four years, and you haven't done anything but two independent movies that did not pay you anything. Why don't you go and try to get on the extras listing?" Mirabelle suggested, her advice stemming from a place of love and concern.

Their exchange, filled with a mix of banter, concern, and earnest suggestions, highlighted the complexities of their relationship. Mirabelle, pragmatic and grounded, sought to steer Michael towards more practical avenues, while Michael, driven by dreams and the allure of stardom, clung to his aspirations with a mix of naivety and determination. This dialogue between siblings encapsulated the tension between realism and idealism, between the safety of the known and the allure of the unknown, a dynamic that defined not only their conversation but also their approach to life's challenges and opportunities.

Michael frowned. "Come on. I played that game for three months, and I got tired of it. All I did was play cards and tell stories about who I would sleep with when I became famous."

"At least you were on movie sets."

"I got kicked off of two for looking at Julia Rogers."

"I still don't believe that story."

Michael shrugged, "Something to do with her finding her character. Something about distracting her."

"What did you do?"

"She couldn't handle being around my awesomeness."

"Is that even a word?"

"If it isn't, it should be."

"I hope that Jack Reynolds doesn't come back here," Mirabelle said, changing the subject.

"What's your issue with Jack Reynolds? He is only the biggest movie star on the planet."

"He hits on me every time he is here. It's getting old."

"He always tips you well."

"That's because he is trying to stop me from suing him for sexual harassment."

Michael grinned, "It must be difficult having girls throw themselves at you."

"You are just as bad as he is, aren't you?"

"I can't even imagine having girls throw themselves at me."

Mirabelle smirked, "You do fine."

Michael sighed, "I could always do better."

"I'm beginning to think that all men are like you."

"When was the last time you had someone in your life?" Michael asked, shifting the conversation back to her.

"I have Buddy."

"Buddy is your cat."

"All I need is Buddy."

"I know how long it's been. I was just seeing if you would tell me."

"It has been at least two years."

"I think it might be closer to three," Michael corrected her.

Mirabelle shrugged, "Two, three, what's the difference?"

"Twelve months."

"I live a very fulfilling life."

"All you do is work and do math problems. Is that a fulfilling life?"

"I also read. When was the last time you read something?"

"Do comic books count?"

Mirabelle couldn't help but laugh, "Well, I suppose they do in your case."

Mirabelle paused and looked up at Michael. "It looks like my break is over."

Chapter 8

AND JUST LIKE JACK

Jack Reynolds entered the lounge, his presence immediately drawing attention. He wore sunglasses and an overcoat, exuding an air of celebrity. As he removed his jacket and placed it on an empty chair, Heather, Tom, and Caleb exchanged glances, their excitement evident.

Jack turned to the group. "I would not recommend going out there. There are paparazzi everywhere."

Heather introduced him with a wave of her hand. "And I give you the star of the movie, Jack Reynolds."

"No need for applause. I am only here for the catering. Oh, and an Oscar."

Heather chimed in, adding to Jack's accolades. "Jack here has won three Oscars."

Jack downplayed his achievements with a humble smile. "But who's counting, right? I mean, after the first one, people are like 'Oh, this guy again.' But I do appreciate the love from my fans." Jack looks around the bar, then states, "I do like this bar, though."

Tom gestured toward the counter. "Caleb has a fan. The waitress Mirabelle over there."

Jack chuckled at the notion. "Isn't it exhausting? I mean, you give, and you give. That girl loves me too. I have been meaning to..."

Heather interrupted. "Jack."

"Yes, ma'am," Jack replied with a half-hearted salute.

"Jack, I was wondering what you thought of the script that I *sent you?"*

"Well, I must be honest with you. I don't really read the scripts, but my assistant Richard read it and told me that I would be a fool to not consider the part of Marlo."

Heather corrected him, clarifying the character's name. "He means Caleb."

Jack scratched his head in confusion. "Are you sure? Because he told me Mario, Marlo, Michael, Martin..."

Heather reiterated, "Caleb."

Jack shrugged with a grin, "Yes, that might be it."

Heather then introduced Jack to Caleb, the writer of the screenplay. As they shook hands, Jack seemed intrigued by Caleb's willingness to share personal his personal story through film.

"Wow. This just blows my mind. So, you're the kind of guy who just lays it all out there?" Jack asked, impressed.

Caleb responded modestly, "I suppose I am."

Heather chimed in, "Caleb has a lot of respectable qualities. Isn't that right?"

"I try," Caleb replied humbly.

Jack nodded. "Well, I can certainly respect that."

Tom interjected, "I respect honesty. I'm Tom Phelps, Caleb's agent.

Tom and Jack exchanged handshakes. Jack couldn't resist making a playful comment. "I didn't know this was an agent thing. I can call mine, and he can be here in ten minutes. You know, that's the funny thing about grossing three billion dollars at the box office; you can get your agent anywhere you want in ten minutes."

Heather interjected, "No, no, this is more of an informal meeting. We aren't signing papers or making promises here. This is more of a meet-and-greet. We wanted to gauge your interest in our project."

Jack hesitated, contemplating whether he should call his agent or not.

Heather gestured toward the chair. "You could call, or you could just take a seat and see where it goes."

Jack relented with a smile. "Well, you do make a convincing argument."

Tom added his perspective on arguments. "Arguments are supposed to be convincing; that's what makes them interesting."

Heather attempted to calm Jack's unease. "Jack, there is no reason to get upset about all of this."

Jack clarified his feelings. "I am not upset. You know I'm just blindsided by all the people here, and the meeting, and I didn't get to bring my agent, and I have all of these people outside trying to take my photograph."

Tom attempted to ease the tension in the room. "Let me get you a drink, Jack."

Their conversation lingered in the air, an exposition of the life lesson woven through their words: that life, in all its chaos and charm, was best navigated with a sense of adventure, the support of those that benefit, and the courage to embrace whatever comes your way.

Chapter 9

CALEB'S DREAM, THE CAVE

The cave's average temperature remained constant at sixty-eight degrees; an unusual anomaly compared to the normal range spanning from ninety to fifty degrees. His recurring dream would unfold identically each time: clad only in a basic loincloth, Caleb would come to consciousness within the cave, the surroundings unchanging even as the faces around him shifted, resembling fleeting mirages.

Sometimes, Caleb's faux therapist would accompany him into the cave, while at other times, he would navigate its depths alone. On this occasion, solitude was his only companion. Slowly, he opened one eye, then the other, his expression shifting from initial disappointment to a sense of resignation. This recurrent predicament had become all too familiar to him.

However, what ensued was anything but typical, as he suddenly found himself engulfed in anguished cries, trembling, and laid bare in his openness. His fears ensnared him, reverting him to the childlike adult he had endeavored to leave behind.

Following the tumultuous storm of his internal childhood, both positive and negative, a serene calm enveloped him. Tears, now dry on his cheeks, were the remnants of a frightened child's vulnerability, leaving behind only his most fundamental, primal fear: the fear of the unknown and of his place within the world. Despite his carefully orchestrated rise to the position of novelist and screenwriter, he now felt adrift in the convoluted recesses of his psyche.

The cave's floor released an unsettling scent, a mixture of chemicals polluting the stagnant air, reminiscent of bleach. Caleb wiped his tears and examined his cavernous environment. A weak light source illuminated a small section of the cave wall, revealing an area marred with chisel marks that bore a cryptic inscription. It displayed "Solitude" above "Divorce" and "Humility."

With increasing desperation, Caleb scrutinized the wall, seeking, like always, any indication of his location, but his search was in vain. He ran his fingers over the drawings carved into the rock, interpreting them as a chronological timeline of his life. From his eighth-grade Spanish class to his swift climb to Hollywood writer, each significant life event was depicted before him. The word "Divorce" stood out prominently, engulfing him in a flood of painful memories and emotional strife.

He found himself in a continuous flux, oscillating between the warm, fond memories of happier times spent with his ex-wife, cherishing the moments of laughter, shared dreams, and tender affections, and the sharp, intense pain she had inflicted upon him, a pain that pierced his heart with the betrayal, misunderstandings, and deep emotional wounds that had eventually led to their separation. This relentless cycle of recalling the joyful, uplifting experiences that once filled his life with light and confronting the harrowing, devastating pain that followed their loss, tethered him to a past filled with both love and anguish, making it a struggle to navigate his present and uncertain about how to move forward into the future.

The inscriptions on the wall overwhelmed Caleb, plunging him into a state of despair and self-perceived failure. His past and future appeared fragmented, leaving him paralyzed by his desolation. Upon encountering the section marked "Finality," he became immobilized, his body stiffening, his movements lethargic. A scream erupted from his throat but was consumed by the cavern's overwhelming silence. Sweat poured from his body.

Each movement was accompanied by excruciating muscle

spasms that sent waves of pain throughout his spine. He fell, crashing face-first onto the ground, whimpering in pain. As he rolled onto his back, he envisioned each cell in his body rebelling, a tumultuous sea of agony flooding his system. The cave toyed with his emotions, pulling him in every direction, leaving him helpless. He longed to stand, to crawl, but his body remained defiantly stationary, his hands grasping at the void in a futile struggle for survival.

Though the cave imprisoned his body, his mind, despite the agony, stayed clear and acutely conscious of the suffering it endured. His thoughts flitted between past loves and regrets, yearning for a brief respite of pure bliss. Then, as suddenly as it had started, the pain subsided. His cells began a process of regeneration, and Caleb felt as though he was undergoing a rebirth. For the ensuing ten minutes, he lay still, curled in a fetal position, hoping the agony would not return.

Slowly, he opened one eye, then the other, surveying his environment for any hint of recognition. A familiar solitary light source from above caught his attention, its radiant glow evoking the gentle, forgiving illumination of a full moon. It enveloped him in warmth and comfort, as if life itself had extended an unforeseen kindness to him.

Then, as suddenly as it had emerged, the light waned, and Caleb closed his eyes once more, surrendering to the silence and darkness that reclaimed the cave.

Chapter 10

THE BAR

Michael maintained his solitary vigil behind the bar, the sparse illumination casting elongated shadows over the sleek surface. Jack Reynolds, perched on a stool, melded into the subdued atmosphere that enveloped the room.

Breaking the stillness, Jack announced, "Yes, I am Jack Reynolds," his voice imbued with a familiarity that assumed recognition. "I assumed you were curious."

With practiced ease, Michael filled a glass with scotch and passed it to Jack, his face betraying no emotion. "I'm aware of who you are, sir," he stated, his voice maintaining a steady cadence.

Jack received the drink, his attention captured by the amber fluid. "Oh, how alluring the poison we find ourselves drawn to," he reflected aloud, his tone introspective.

"Sir?" Michael inquired.

"I'm merely appreciating the dynamic between myself and the drink. It's often the minor pleasures that bring us joy," Jack elaborated, his gaze fixed on the glass.

"Undoubtedly, sir."

Curiosity piqued, Jack queried, "You know...What's your name?"

"Michael. I've spent four years here, working with my sister."

Jack arched an eyebrow. "You provided a succinct autobiography in response to a simple inquiry. Is that a common practice for you?"

"Not typically," Michael confessed, a hint of amusement evident.

"Now that we've clarified your unusual practices, let's shift to a more uplifting subject. Michael, I want to assure you that I am no different from you," Jack ventured, leaning forward.

"And how is that?"

"Ever find yourself in a dream, locked in a gaze with a captivating woman, her eyes reflecting a deep, unwavering infatuation?"

"Indeed," Michael acknowledged, sharing a personal insight for perhaps the first time.

"I experience that reality daily, while you merely dream it. Do you see our common ground?"

"May I offer you another drink?"

Jack polished off his drink and extended the empty glass towards Michael as Mirabelle made her entrance.

"I'm of the belief that as long as the studio foots the bill for this celebration, it's my duty to ensure your glass remains full." Michael topped off Jack's glass once more.

"I admire your approach, Michael. It's refreshing to encounter someone who knows..." Jack's sentence trailed off as he became aware of Mirabelle's presence.

Directing his full attention to Mirabelle, Jack inquired boldly, "Would you like to accompany me home tonight?"

In the dimly lit ambiance of the bar, the interplay between Jack and Mirabelle wove a tapestry of unresolved tension and unyielding defiance. Mirabelle's immediate rejection, succinctly voiced with a "No thanks," set a stark boundary against Jack's presumptive allure.

Jack, taken aback, countered with incredulity, "No? No one says no to me," his voice a mixture of disbelief and inflated self-regard, *challenging Mirabelle's firm stance.*

Unruffled, Mirabelle shot back, "I have said 'no' to you roughly two hundred and four times tonight so far," her words sharpened by the weariness of repeated rebuffs.

Jack, unfazed and buoyed by a misplaced sense of inevitability, ventured, "Oh, you are a woman that I will someday enjoy the nectar of," only to be met with Mirabelle's unwavering rebuttal, "I am pretty sure you won't."

As the conversation deepened, Jack sought to invoke sympathy for his professed heartache, a ploy met with Mirabelle's discerning skepticism. "Who broke your heart this time?" she prodded; her tone laden with the anticipation of a rehearsed tale.

Jack, attempting a connection, confessed, "Oh, it was the sweet angel on the set...she kind of looked like you, that might have been why I was so into her," a revelation that elicited from Mirabelle a dismissive, "Well, that is a shame, isn't it."

Seeking affirmation of his identity, Jack queried, "You do know who I am, right?"

Mirabelle responded with an overwhelming sense of sarcasm, "Of course I do, and as much as it pains me to keep saying no to you, I will continue to say no to you."

Their dialogue continued to unravel as Michael watched from afar, with Jack expressing a stubborn determination to gain Mirabelle's favor, a resolve she countered with the mention of her ongoing romantic commitment, "I have had the same boyfriend for the last six months."

Even the invocation of Caleb, the creative mind behind Jack's latest cinematic endeavor, failed to shift Jack's perception. Her assurance that "Oh, but he is better in real life" clashed with Jack's boastful claim of his own acting prowess, underscored by his three Academy Awards.

Jack's assertion of his ability to mimic Caleb, "I am pretty sure that I could fool you," was quickly deflated by Mirabelle's pointed critique of his ego, a trait she viewed not as confidence but as excess, "You obviously don't have a lack of ego."

Their exchange veered into a discussion on the nature of Jack's ego, with him viewing it as proportional confidence, while Mirabelle remained unswayed.

Jack, in a bid for empathy, reiterated his claim of emotional turmoil, "I have a broken heart though. You wouldn't shy away from a man so broken, would you?"

Mirabelle wearily recognized this all-too-familiar narrative. "You tell me that same story every time you are in here."

"Oh, but this time it is true."

"I don't believe you."

"Because my movie wrapped today, and I am a man without a script, I am here wounded for you."

Yet, as she prepared to exit, laden with a tray of beverages, Mirabelle's brief acknowledgment of Jack's frankness, despite her doubts about his genuineness, offered a fleeting moment of understanding in their otherwise contentious interaction.

After Mirabelle walked away, Jack, perhaps seeking a measure of solace or comprehension from Michael in the silence that followed, leaned toward the bartender. The remnants of their verbal joust lingered in the air, entombed in the complex dance of words and wills that had transpired, leaving both parties ensnared in a stalemate of emotions and intentions.

Jack, leaning over the bar with a hint of mischief in his eyes, regaled Michael with a tale from the set of his latest film. "So, I open the trailer naked with a bow around, you know my...my..." He trailed off, leaving the conclusion hanging in the air.

"Your member," Michael supplied, unfazed by Jack's theatrics.

"Ok, let's go with member...So I feel this heat between us because we have these love scenes together, and because of the method acting, I am a little involved in the story and the character and what the character would do..." *Jack explained, his enthusiasm evident as he plunged deeper into his process.*

"So, what happened?" *Michael prodded.*

"I am in the character, and it encompasses my being. I am in deep; I sleep and breathe Caleb Garcia. I live this guy, I am this guy, and this woman is Caleb's wife..."

"Ok, so you are in character, you are walking, talking, and being this man..."

"No, you don't get it. I no longer exist. Caleb exists; I am just the vessel the character comes out of. Well, one day, I am naked with only a bow tie on my member, as you put it, and I am not shy because this is my, Caleb's, wife, and I feel comfortable with it, so the day the movie wrapped—"

"Didn't the movie wrap yesterday?" *Michael interjected.*

"It may have," *Jack conceded, his timeline slightly ambiguous.*

"So, this all happened yesterday?"

"What are you trying to say?" *Jack detected a hint of skepticism in Michael's tone.*

"The way you talk about it, you make it sound like it was years *ago, and it was something like twelve hours ago."*

"Can I finish my story, or should I stop talking?"

"No, go on," Michael encouraged, genuinely interested in hearing the conclusion.

"Veronica, that's her name. Well, the actress, her name is Veronica. The character is Renée," Jack mused aloud, pondering the duality of the actress and her character. "Should I call her Renée or Veronica?" he questioned himself before continuing. "Okay, so I go to her trailer, and I am in my 'outfit.' I imagine opening her trailer door and her looking at me and the two of us making passionate love together. I imagine her response, her looking at me and telling me how she has been waiting for this her whole life and I am all she has ever wanted. You see, in the back of my mind, I know I am Jack Reynolds, the actor, but I feel like I am Caleb. It was a very confusing time for me. I was Caleb, but I was conscious that I was there, also. I saw what I was doing but I really didn't know what I was doing because I was passionate about love, and I knew she loved me."

After a pause, Jack revealed the climax of his tale. "I open the door, and she is on the phone with her agent, producer, boyfriend, girlfriend, who really knows. She is half in wardrobe and half in her home clothes, you know, because it's the end of the day. She looks up at me, and her face drops. I stare right into her soul, drop my pants, and yell 'Supersex.'"

"Did she ask for the soup?" Michael quipped, lightening the mood with a joke.

Jack paused, the gravity of the moment settling in. "No, she called security, and I was escorted off of the set. I was told I was done filming, so there was no point in me staying. People I loved turned on me because of this one thing. People looked at me like

I was a freak. I just wanted to prove my love to her. I was so convinced that she and I should be together, not the me and her in front of you—the characters. The characters onscreen. I was lost."

"So, what are you going to do?"

"I think I'm done," Jack muttered to himself, a sense of resignation in his voice.

"What do you mean?"

"I am going to leave this town."

"Jack, I don't...I don't understand. How can you just walk away?" Michael's voice barely hid his shock, his admiration for Jack evident in his wide, questioning eyes.

Jack's laugh was bitter, a sound more akin to a scoff. "You think this is about walking away, Michael? This...This is about survival. It's about not losing myself to a character so completely that I can't find my way back. Have you ever felt that? So lost in a role that you forget who you are?"

Michael shook his head, his confusion clear. "No, I can't say I have."

"Of course, you haven't," Jack snapped, his frustration boiling over. "And you won't understand, not really. It's one thing to play a part, to step into someone else's shoes for a while. But it's another to look in the mirror and not recognize the person staring back at you. I became a vessel, Michael. Just a shell for whatever character I was playing, with no control over who I was anymore."

"But you're one of the best actors in town," Michael protested, his voice tinged with disbelief. "You have a gift, Jack. People would kill for your success."

"Success?" Jack's laugh was hollow this time. "Is that what

you think this is about? Success? I'm not an actor, Michael. I'm a parrot. A clothes hanger for costumes. I recite lines. That's it. There's no art in what I do, not anymore. It's all just...noise."

Michael fell silent, unable to find the words to counter Jack's despair. He watched as Jack paced near the counter; each step heavy with unspoken regrets.

"I used to do theater, you know," Jack continued, his voice softer now, reflective. "There was a magic to it, a connection with the audience you can't find anywhere else. But I chased the dream, the Hollywood dream, thinking it was the pinnacle of our craft. And now...I wonder if I was just running from the real work, the real art of acting."

"You moved here for opportunity, right? To be an actor?" Michael finally found his voice again, his curiosity piqued.

Jack nodded, a ghost of a smile on his lips. "Opportunity. But that's just it, isn't it? Opportunity is a double-edged sword. It's the same thing that drives people to greatness or madness. You take a chance, you pretend to be something you're not, and suddenly, you're lost, hacking away at the very essence of who you thought you were."

Michael frowned. "That's...that's a bit intense, Jack."

Jack stopped pacing and looked at Michael, a fierce determination in his eyes. "But that's the point, isn't it? To be great, to really make something of yourself in this industry, you can't just sit back and wait for it to come to you. You have to go out there, pound the pavement, show them who you are and what you can do. And maybe, just maybe, you'll light up the stage, own it in a way that no one else can. That's what it means to be an actor, to marry the idea of this craft and make it your life."

Michael listened, the weight of Jack's words settling over him like a cloak. "So, what are you saying? That I should just...give up?"

"No," *Jack said firmly, his gaze unwavering.* "I'm saying you should fight. Fight for every role, every opportunity, no matter how small. Make it yours. And one day, you'll be the one people look up to, asking how to make it in this crazy world."

A silence fell between them, heavy with the gravity of their conversation. Michael looked at Jack, a new resolve in his eyes. Clearly Jack had given this speech before, and it was more for his pleasure than bestowing any real wisdom.

"I'm here to be an actor, Jack. Just like you."

The tension in the room thickened as Jack met his gaze, almost palpable as they navigated through the murky waters of fame.

"Well, not exactly like you, but..." *Michael's voice trailed off, his gaze shifting uneasily under Jack's intense scrutiny.*

Jack, visibly taken aback, paused, the weight of his experiences pressing down on him. "Like me? Like me, huh?" *His voice, tinged with a mix of shock and a bitter realization, echoed in the cramped space.* "Let me tell you about my life. I've been divorced twice. I've been adored by people who I do not know, who call me by my characters' names, not mine. My name is Jack, not Tom Kelly or Walter Jenkins. These were characters I played."

The silence that followed was heavy, filled with unspoken words and thoughts left to linger in the air. Jack's revelation was a glimpse into the solitude often accompanying fame, a solitude that Michael had yet to understand or experience.

"You know that every person I meet thinks they know me already?" *Jack continued; his voice soft but laced with an edge of frustration.*

"What do you mean?" Michael inquired, genuinely puzzled by the notion.

Jack sighed, a sound of weariness and resignation. "What I'm telling you is that every day, I'm thrust into the homes of people who think they know who I am. So, all my relationships are ruined. I meet a pretty girl, and she doesn't want to love me or be with me; she wants to be with the movie star. I'm not even a real person anymore. I'm a product."

Michael, unable to hide his skepticism, countered, "A product that makes you very wealthy."

Jack shook his head, his expression somber. "Money cannot buy you happiness."

"It can buy you joy until happiness comes along, right?"

Jack looked at him, bewildered by his misunderstanding. "What are you talking about?"

"You're a multimillionaire. I made twenty grand last year, and you're going to tell me that it's so bad to be rich and famous? I guess you can look down on the poor people in life. I find it surprising that you need to try and impress me with your talk about acting, how it's so difficult to have money and to have people love you for just being on the television or the big screen."

"Listen," Jack interjected, his tone firm yet weary, "it's not all puppy dogs and rainbows on this side of the bar. Whether you're a bartender or a movie star, it's all the same; it's all part of the problem."

"Are you talking about communism now?" Michael asked, confusion etched across his face.

Jack let out a frustrated sigh. "No, no, listen. I'm just saying that we're both the same. We're both on the same plane, flying to the same destination."

"What does that mean?"

It meant that beneath the veneer of fame and fortune, beneath the roles and accolades, they were both human, navigating through life's complexities, searching for meaning, connection, and authenticity. Jack's journey had taught him the hard lessons of identity and isolation, lessons Michael had yet to learn.

The room fell into a long pause, a silence that seemed to stretch indefinitely between Jack and Michael, each man wrapped in his own thoughts until Jack broke the silence with a proposition that was both generous and desperate. "I will pay you to go back to Seattle and do plays. How much do you think it would cost me to do that for you? You see, I have the money. If I can save one soul, then I have done something good."

Michael's response was immediate and resolute. "I don't want to go back to Seattle. I am here to make it."

Jack sighed, took a sip of his abandoned drink, and sat back down to collect his thoughts. He decided to try once more to change the young man's mind. He began to tell Michael a story he once heard from a famous actor advising him to return to Miami, his hometown. Jack leaned back, a wry smile playing on his lips. "You know," he started, his voice taking on a reflective tone, "The Denver Philharmonic Orchestra, those folks dedicated to their music, found themselves in a bit of a bind once. They were on a routine flight to a gig, when suddenly, they had to make an emergency landing in this nowhere town between Denver and Chicago. Imagine that: a group of artists thrown into everyday life, miles away from their destination."

He paused, chuckling at the thought before continuing. "So, there they were, dealing with the hassle of renting cars in pouring rain. It was miserable, cold, and wet: a real test of their dedication. But it's in those moments, you know, that you see what you're really made of. These artists, they live for their music, not knowing where it'll take them next."

Jack's eyes twinkled as he recounted the musicians finding refuge in a local bar, looking like drowned rats. "And then, they see this family, all warm and cozy, laughing and enjoying their dinner together. It was such a stark contrast to their own situation. Made them think, you know, about the choices they'd made, choosing music over everything else."

He leaned in, lowering his voice as if sharing a secret. "The silence among them was deafening until one of the percussionists just said, 'Screw that.' And together, like a well-rehearsed piece, they all said, 'Fuck them.' Not out of bitterness, but as a declaration of their own path, a rejection of mediocrity."

Jack's story took a deeper turn as he explained how these artists had chosen a life far removed from conventional happiness, embracing the sacrifices required for their art. "They're creators, living for something beyond the mundane. It's not an easy path, but it's theirs."

Finishing his tale, Jack looked at Michael with a sense of earnestness. "This story, it's about more than just a stranded orchestra. It's a lesson about what it really means to live for your art, to choose a path that's not just about seeking comfort or security. It's about being true to yourself, even when it means walking away from what others might see as a 'normal' life."

There was a long moment of silence after Jack finished his story. He sat back, seemingly proud of the lesson he'd imparted, while Michael couldn't help but feel a mixture of awe and confusion. His words had opened a window to a world Michael was still *struggling to understand, a world where the art and the artist's dedication to it transcended the conventional aspirations of life.*

"But why?" Michael asked, drawn into Jack's narrative.

"Because the family chooses to be mediocre while the musicians are creating," Jack explained. "They get to be part of something big every day, creating, while others are content with the sameness of daily life. If you want acting, go back to Seattle. If you want the truth, go back to Seattle. But if you're going to be an arrogant movie star, then you're in the right place."

Jack's gaze swept the room, his thoughts on the industry's superficiality. "Some of the best movies are made when actors forget about their agents, publicists, and life coaches. I am who I am because I have at least ten people working for me."

Michael tried to clarify his ambitions. "It's not that I want to make it big, it's just that I want to work on characters that…"

Jack cut him off. "When you're a movie star, it's all gone. The characters are clouded by explosions on the screen. Hollywood has script doctors who add in more sex and violence, forgetting the art of telling a moving story."

"So how do we—"

"Listen…Shhh, shh…You hear that?" Jack whispered, an air of mystery enveloping his words.

"Hear what?"

"That sound."

"What are you talking about?"

"That," Jack said, pausing for effect, "is the sound of all the people who really care about me."

Chapter 11

WHY FRED?

Fred Williams was a middle-aged man. He stood an imposing six feet four inches and hunched his shoulders when he walked. His posture was poor, and his weight was high. His cholesterol had tipped the scale at a whopping 300. He felt bad about his appearance and his weight yet did very little about it. He constantly planned diets for Monday but would find a reason to quit after 10am. His work history moved him all around the continental United States. He had worked in Sacramento, Seattle, Portland, Miami, Norfolk, Virginia, and Denver in the previous five years. He was a Disc Jockey, working in various formats throughout his career, but had recently been forced into a scandalous talk show. His program director a year prior had sat him down and told him to titillate the audience to increase ratings. He discovered his inner loudmouth and began spouting insults right into the microphone. He went from second to last in the ratings to number three. He parted his hair in the middle, which made his imposing figure seem larger. He slept in 700 thread count sheets in an apartment that had been featured in many local magazines as an example of an incredible view of downtown Los Angeles.

Throughout his distinguished career, Fred underwent the dissolution of three marriages, yet he persistently nurtured affection for his inaugural spouse, who severed ties upon discovering his indiscretion with the cleaning staff. Lacking genuine attraction to the cleaner, his motivation had been driven by a desire to embody the virile image he portrayed over the radio waves. The loss of his first love grieved him deeply, though he soon found solace in another union. His subsequent wife, Maria, an avid listener of his broad-

cast, felt a connection to Fred as he shared his solitude and marital woes on the air, leading to their swift marriage six weeks after she called in.

Maria's exit from Fred's life was precipitated by the return of her erstwhile spouse from prison, barely a year into her marriage to Fred. This departure scarcely affected him; he regarded Maria as a temporary diversion from his enduring affection for his initial wife. Following the dissolution with Maria, Fred embarked on a reckless journey, indulging in promiscuous encounters that culminated in an HPV diagnosis, marking a phase of self-destruction fueled by his successive personal tumults. Thereafter, he had boxes of condoms throughout his house which—an eyesore for any visitors yet representative of his respect for other humans.

Fred would sweat the moment the microphone was on until he would spin the next record or fire a commercial break. He would spend most of his time during the commercial breaks smoking cigarettes or marijuana. He attempted to cloud his tortured mind with relaxing devices. He had recently been prescribed valium but hated taking medications. He also hated himself. Self-loathing ran rampant in his family.

Fred's third wife had been a Miss Ecuador. Fred met her at a cocktail party hosted by the owner of the radio station. Fred was the only one at the party who spoke Spanish, a language his mother had forced on him as a child. Fred hated speaking Spanish, as he saw it as a mutt language, but with Carlotta, it seemed beautiful and exotic. Their romance was reported in local media. Their divorce was covered by the same reporters six weeks after their marriage. Carlotta decided that she wanted to be with the local professional football player instead of the middle-aged radio loudmouth. Awkwardly, Fred was asked to interview the football player shortly after, during which he broke down and confronted the player about his infidelity. Fred was fired from the show during the commercial break. He then moved to Los Angeles.

In Los Angeles, Fred had been given the figurative keys to the afternoon drive time shift at a local talk radio station. He turned a restrictive four hours into an exciting and positive show without pushing the envelope too far. He was not hated by management but was rather regarded as a hero.

For the most part, Fred was embarrassed by his sexual conquests. On the rare occasion that he would have a visitor to his apartment, the visitor would find herself with a large stack of dollars in her pocket and disappointment on her mind. He found it difficult to meet people. Yet every third Sunday, he would find himself driving down the same road, stopping by the same, lone, burnt-out streetlamp. The road promised nothing but an empty temporary companionship.

One day, after a particularly disappointing escapade, Fred sat in the radio booth in a daze. Board operator Elvin Jasper tapped on the window after a good three seconds of "dead air." Fred snapped to attention and dug into one of his signature diatribes. He bitched about taxes and religion for ten minutes until his next break mark. Once he fired the first set of commercials, the energy seemed to be sucked out of him. It was as if all his self-esteem and self-importance had been stolen from him. He blamed it on his recent rehab endeavor and denouncement of drugs.

Fred stared at the computer screen looking over potential callers. There was Terry, the caller who always wanted to talk about how terrible the Governor was, John, who wanted to discuss how landlords are the devil, and Chritina, who wanted to ask if she saw Fred under a broken lamppost the Sunday prior. No one seemed of interest to him, so he dumped them all by turning the phone bank from on to off. He stared out into the wilderness of his own mind, *planning his next move.*

Elvin entered the room and waited for Fred to say something, but he was only silent. Elvin gathered portions of the newspaper while Fred kept staring. The commercial break was coming to a close, and Fred whispered inaudibly to himself. Elvin looked at him as if Fred had lost his mind. Once Elvin left the room, Fred stood up and locked the door behind him.

Fred was now completely alone. He stared out the window for the final sixty-second commercial spot as he had done for the previous four. Once the microphone was active, Fred leaned in close to the microphone and discussed a documentary he had recently seen about the benefits of sleeping more than eight hours a night. The phones lit up and, following a long-winded dialogue about how Hollywood had lost its edge by only funding safe movies without real writers, he began answering the phone."

"Hot 88, this is Fred Williams."

"Hi, my name is John, and I have to tell you that...You know when...I just feel like..."

Fred hung up on him without batting an eye. He had very little patience for people that could not come up with a viable point within five seconds.

Two hours later, Fred's shift was over, and he exited the building holding his head low as if carrying heavy mental anguish. He found himself walking into an Alcoholics Anonymous meeting, even though he was not an alcoholic; he was a drug addict. *Is marijuana even a drug?* he thought to himself. The meeting was held at a local office building, dark and nondescript. He walked in and sat near the backs of the room, trying not to make a scene. He was grasping at straws, searching for any outlet to verbalize his pain. He had tried therapists, but he felt as though they were paid to listen, and he didn't receive a hug afterward, just a bill. He later rationalized that marijuana was his fall-back drug and that he had a history with other powdered substances.

Fred rubbed his hands together for thirty minutes, waiting to be called by the meeting leader. Fred felt tired and beaten by the system. Over the last few months, he had found it easier to say he was an alcoholic and not, in reality, a run-of-the-mill pot smoker.

"Hello, my name is Fred, and I am an alcoholic. It has been six weeks since my last drink, and I feel like the pain will never go away. I feel a complete emptiness in my soul and my mind. I cannot shake the demons that seemingly surround my every step—"

Fred was interrupted by another patron.

"Wait, are you Fred Williams from Hot 88? Hey, everyone, this is the guy from Hot 88! I love this guy!"

Fred promptly exited the meeting.

The next morning, at 8am, Fred lifted his head from the pillow and pulled on his running shoes. Once he exited his front door, he noticed a small briefcase on his doorstep. It was labeled with his name and address. He looked around but did not see anyone in the hallway. He lightly kicked it, examining it and measuring its fragility.

Fred stared at the briefcase for a few minutes, decided to scratch his morning jog from his to-do list, and placed it in his apartment. He smiled for a brief minute, admiring that he had scratched his morning job off his list for six months straight now. He shaved and showered, all the while thinking about the briefcase's contents.

After Fred stared at the briefcase for another minute or two, he placed it on the dining table and attempted to pry it open with *a butter knife. His cell phone rang, startling him.*

He searched for a cordless phone in the house but could not find one.

Twenty minutes later, the briefcase was open, revealing a thick stack of papers. Fred closely examined each sheet. There were thousands. Each page Fred read detailed the everyday events of his life, beginning on his sixteenth birthday and ending the day before receiving the briefcase.

Fred read about his twenty-first birthday and his twenty-eighth birthday. He read about his marriages and divorces. He found himself reading specific pages that chronicled days he did not recall. However, due to their complete accuracy, he found them completely believable.

He noticed one piece of paper with the inscription August 8, 2018. He proceeded to read.

Mr. Williams was seen in the hallway of his apartment at 0800 in the morning until 0806. He then re-entered his apartment, showered, and exited his apartment at 0945. He went to the grocery store and was viewed by many patrons looking at containers of milk, measuring their expiration dates. He eventually purchased a candy bar, an energy drink, an orange, and two packs of gum. Mr. Williams then drove to his therapist "Dr. Hayes" and discussed his childhood. Once Mr. Williams exited his office, Dr. Hayes made a phone call to local newspaper owner "Scott Wheeler" and attempted to sell the notes that he had written about Mr. Williams. No deal was made, as Mr. Wheeler was contacted by our office and the deal was broken. Mr. Williams arrived at 6800 Firecrest Drive (Hot 88 Studios) and discussed local news and politics for four hours. At 1923 hours, Mr. Williams exited the building and was approached by one Kelvin Stewart, a student from the local university for an autograph. Mr. Williams obliged the request and arrived home at 2006. From 2040 to 2300, he watched television, retired to the bedroom, then fell asleep at 2341.

Fred looked around his apartment, exhaustively searching for a camera, but did not find one. He returned to the pages and read through many more days. On some pages were red marks lined through entire sections of copy. Fred examined these pages carefully and placed them in a separate pile. Fred nervously looked out his window but only saw a group of children making their way to school. He frantically searched for a camera once more, but, again, came up empty-handed.

He yelled at the pages as if they had imposed on his life. He screamed, "Why are you doing this?" as if the papers were a human being with real emotion and character.

After three hours of rummaging through the pages, he placed them all neatly inside the briefcase and left for work. He locked not just the main fastener but the deadbolt and hid it in what he considered a safe place: under his bed. Then, he left his apartment.

When Fred arrived at work, he was welcomed by a large group of people who were celebrating the upcoming premiere of the docuseries On the Set. He attempted to break through the crowd, but the celebration impeded his travels. He eventually made it to his office with stale streamers covering his face and shoulders. He violently shook them off his torso and hair and picked up the phone. He dialed furiously.

"Dr. Webber, I need to talk to you. No, no, today...No, not my childhood. We're going to have to put that aside for now. How about we worry about...I know I'm behind on payments...Listen, I need to talk to someone...Why? Why?!"

Fred slammed the phone on the receiver. A moment passed, then an intern walked by. Fred opened his door to lash out at the intern, but standing there was Caleb Garcia, his long-lost friend.

Chapter 12

THE BAR REVISITED

Jack and Michael sat in the dimly lit corner of a bar, nursing their drinks as the world outside buzzed with the oblivious energy of a nighttime crowd. The clink of glasses and low hum of evening chatter formed a backdrop to their dialogue, a conversation that analyzed the realms of success, dependency, and the stark realities of human relationships.

"There's this economics term," Jack began, swirling his drink absently and subconsciously rolling his wrist in circles. "It's called the law of diminishing returns. It states that no matter how much input you place into any one system, the output will be the same. Thus, people only care about the output, not the sheer volume of input."

Michael looked at him, a soft smile playing on his lips. "I'm sure that people care about you."

Jack scoffed, a bitter edge to his laugh. "What, my agent, my ex-wives, my publicist, my managers?"

"Sure."

"They all live off of me."

"That can't be true."

"Oh, I assure you that it is true. And what makes it worse is that I let them. I ask them to be in my life and then I pay them to be in my life. That is a pretty good relationship on their side, isn't it?" Jack's voice carried a mix of irony and resignation.

"I suppose." Michael stuttered.

"You suppose?"

"I suppose that if you are emotionally satisfied living a life where you have become a source of wealth, then that can happen."

Jack signaled for a refill, his mood seemingly darkening with each sip of his drink. Michael took the glass, refilled it with a bottle at the table, and handed it back to Jack, who took a deep gulp before continuing.

"Did you know I am a bit of a history buff—though I still don't know why they call it 'history buff.' They should call it 'how the world works and why your future is going to be terrible.'" He paused, gathering his thoughts. "Ok, in 1966, Muhammad Ali, who was the heavyweight champion at the time, decided that he did not want to be in the army due to some draft issue. So, he gets banned from boxing in 1967, and all his friends leave him. They all just go away. Poof, they're gone. But when he is reinstated in 1970, everyone comes back."

Jack's voice grew more intense, his words painting a picture of solitude amidst success. "Because they were all leeches. That is what my life is like. If I moved on to something else and stopped making films, I would have no one. They are all just leeches waiting for the scraps I leave them. I am more alone with success than I ever was without it."

Michael remained silent for a moment, considering Jack's words. "I don't think that's really the case," he finally said, his voice a mixture of optimism and concern.

"I am telling you, it is," Jack insisted, "I would much rather do..." He paused, lost in thought, before a memory seemed to strike him. "In high school, there was this exercise that I think everyone does, you know, it's like one of those..." He gestured with air quotes, "If you could do anything, any profession, and not have to worry about *the amount of money you were paid, if all that was already taken care of and you could do anything for the fun of just doing it—what would you do?"*

Jack downed the remainder of his drink in one swift motion, a gesture of finality. Michael, ever the attentive listener, refilled Jack's glass once more, an unspoken symbol of their prolonged discussion.

"So, what would you have done?" Michael asked, genuinely curious.

Jack hesitated, then with a level of honesty that seemed to cost him, admitted, "I would have been a nurse."

"Like a male nurse?"

"Yes, there's nothing wrong with that. You help people and are like a liaison for the doctor. Like a flight attendant for the sick."

"You can still do that, you know."

"I can't be a nurse now," Jack dismissed the idea with a wave of his hand.

"You have the money to do whatever you want; you can move to a different place and live out your dreams. You could even get a job with little to no real responsibility."

"I am trained for nothing," Jack countered.

"I am sure you could go to school to learn how to do something."

"I'm thirty-five. I'm not sure there are a whole lot of jobs that involve hitting your mark, wearing makeup, and crying on cue," Jack retorted.

"Maybe a clown."

"Yeah, maybe. Or maybe I just move to some faraway land without paparazzi and live a totally boring and uninspired life where I wait to die."

"I just don't get it, man."

"Objection, counselor," Jack quipped, a brief smile flickering across his face.

"Sustained."

"What are you talking about?"

"I am talking about the pain, man."

"The pain?"

"I am talking about moving on. More like running towards the light."

"Are you sad or depressed? Something like that?"

"It's not that I am sad or depressed, or that I am going to tear up over here. I am not going to commit to doing something without thoughtfully thinking it over first. I don't just jump into things without wrapping my mind around the choices in front of me. I am saying that I have become one of those people. You know, one of the people who looks down on unsuccessful people and feels bad for them?"

"Wait. Do you feel bad for me?"

"I feel nothing for you, man. The fact that we are having this conversation is actually me doing a favor for you, and it really shouldn't be that way. I shouldn't feel this contempt and disregard for other people," Jack said, lying to himself.

"You have lost your connection with the rest of the world. Is that what you're trying to say?"

"I am trying to say that I am as flawed as you are, yet for some reason, I look down on you," Jack confessed, his voice carrying a weight of self-awareness. "I look at you and think that you are not as good as I am. I am on billboards, and you are working at the bar. This bar where you wait for people to give you money for their poison."

"Wait. Do you pity me?" Michael asked, a note of incredulity in his voice that couldn't hide the sting of the implication.

There was a beat, a palpable tension that seemed to stretch between them before Jack finally responded, "Pity is such a strong word."

"What word would you use?"

"I suppose it comes down to feeling sorry for you,"

"I have a decent life; there is no reason to feel sorry for me."

"You just don't get it. It is more of a pain that I feel for you for wanting what I clearly don't want."

"But why don't you want it?"

"The exact reason you do want it."

"I want it for the fame and the success."

"Those are two opposing forces. You see, you can be successful building a chair. You wake up and look at a piece of wood and say, 'I am going to make something out of that.' I look at words on paper and say I am going to make something out of that, it is no different. I create a character out of thin air, just like a skillfully crafted chair maker builds out of pine or birch," Jack mused. After a pause, he added with a hint of humor, "I really have no idea how chairs are made."

"I'm sure they're no longer made from hand."

"You are missing the point entirely. I want you to understand that success is in your head. You can live and breathe success every day. You can wake up one morning and decide that on that particular day you are going to run outside or go to the park. I, on the other hand, look outside my window and hope the paparazzi fall out of the tree they climbed to get a snapshot of me from across the street."

"Why can't you just go outside, give them their photographs, and move on?"

"Because it never ends. They follow me and they take pictures of me all the time. If I have dinner with anyone, I am getting married to them or I am having an affair. If I have a bad hair day, they might report that I am wearing a wig. It's an awful way to live life. Have you ever seen the movie The Wall?" Jack inquired, drawing a parallel to a tale of isolation and scrutiny.

"About the guy who shaved off his eyebrows?"

"It is about a bit more than that, but...It goes back to my original question. You need to know if you want to be an artist or a movie star."

"I don't see why those have to be mutually exclusive."

"You are either for the art or the wealth. Because wealth spoils the art, but art never spoils the wealth. In fact, art is the wealth if you play it right."

"I just think that you are going through a dark period in your life."

"I have no excuse."

Michael, seeking to shift the mood, walked to the bar, then returned, bringing a bottle of scotch with him. He sat down, opened the bottle, and filled up both their glasses. "I think a little scotch will do wonders," he proposed, offering solace in the form of a shared drink.

"Do you even hear what I'm saying?"

"I do," Michael assured him.

"No, I don't think you're listening to me."

"What would give you that impression?"

"Well, the fact that you are daydreaming while I am speaking. Your generation is full of daydreamers, but no one that wants to actually do the work."

"I work here. I was serving you just a few hours ago," Michael pointed out, a reminder of his commitment and presence in the moment.

"Life is pain, and I want you to know that every day I feel as though I am getting punched in the face," Jack shared, his metaphor a stark depiction of his daily struggle.

"You know there are bigger problems to have than being too famous," Michael responded, trying to offer perspective.

"There are many problems that I see with the world. Even so, this is not how I wanted it to turn out when it all began," Jack confessed.

"And it is not real now?" Michael asked.

"The relationships I have are the same ones I had in high school," Jack revealed.

"Isn't that the standard though?" Michael replied.

"How do you figure that?" Jack asked, his question hanging in the air like a challenge.

"We have established ground rules for the way that people interact with each other. They place us all in the same groups they did in high school. You have the jocks, the nerds, the guys with a motorcycle, the drama nerds; it is all the same,"

"Maybe it shouldn't be," Jack mused.

"If this was a quality-of-life-based society, we would have less divorce, but that is just the way it is. People emulate the interactions that they see in the movies; they base their entire lives on them."

"Is that what you see?"

"That is what everyone sees. You think that people don't look up to you, do you?"

"Of course they do," Jack admitted, not without a hint of pride.

"They want to be like the characters you represent, not the person you truly are. If you showed who you truly were, no one would respect you," Michael asserted.

"Of course they would," Jack argued.

As Michael refilled Jack's drink, the conversation took a more personal turn. "You think that people want to take pictures with you because you are a humanitarian?"

"You don't understand how this game is played," Jack retorted.

"I do know that I moved out here to be an actor, and you have ruined that with your fake tan and pearly white teeth."

"You have no idea."

Michael finally met his patient point and boiled over with "Oh, I think I do. I think you showed up in Los Angeles which is not the person that now stands in front of me. You no longer respect yourself. So here is what is going to happen. You are going to finish your drink and leave this bar. Shortly following that, I am going to walk out of this bar and move back to Seattle to have a real life. More specifically, to never have to deal with another movie star clown such as yourself; you ruin everything you touch due to your own narcissism," Michael declared, his decision firm and final.

"As long as the results are the same, I don't care how you came to the conclusion," Jack responded, his voice cold and detached.

"As well you shouldn't," Michael agreed, his tone equally frosty.

"And we should celebrate that decision!" Jack exclaimed, attempting to inject a note of levity into the heavy atmosphere.

"It is a decision that is not to be celebrated. It is an ultimate realization that you should have figured out a long time ago. There is no creativity here," Michael stated.

"Pour me another drink. I have saved another confused soul," Jack said, attempting to reclaim some semblance of control over the conversation.

"Do you really think you saved me?" Michael asked, his question hanging between them, a final challenge to Jack's self-perception and the very nature of their conversation.

At this point the bar was nearly empty, the earlier cacophony of laughter and chatter now replaced by the soft, intermittent clinks of glass and the low, muffled sounds of a city winding down.

"More than anyone saved me," Jack confessed, his voice carrying a mix of defiance and vulnerability.

"You have terrible friends then," Michael retorted, his words sharp, yet not without a hint of concern.

Jack couldn't help but chuckle, a sound tinged with both irony and sadness. "I think I mentioned that before," he acknowledged.

As the night drew to its inevitable close, the two men found themselves at a crossroads, both literally and metaphorically. For Jack, the evening had been a rare opportunity to peel back the layers *of his carefully curated image, revealing the doubts and fears that lurked behind the mask. For Michael, it was a moment of realization, a glimpse into the hollowness that could accompany success when it was measured solely by fame and fortune. Their conversation, a blend of confrontation and confession, had laid bare the complexities of their lives, leaving them to ponder the price of their dreams and the value of the authenticity they had sacrificed along the way.*

Chapter 13

FRED AND CALEB

The acquisition of the first three episodes of the show by Tom, Caleb's agent, had been a bittersweet victory. Tom, ever the pragmatist, had seen it as an opportunity for reflection and perhaps a catalyst for change. For Fred and Caleb, however, the episodes were a window into a past that felt both intimately familiar and painfully distant. As they watched, the memories of their aspirations and the harsh realities that followed played out before them, a narrative juxtaposed against the backdrop of their current, more modest circumstances.

The dimly lit room, with its worn furnishings and the pervasive sense of unfulfilled potential, became a theater of their shared experiences. The shadows cast by the television light seemed to dance around them, mocking echoes of the dreams they had once chased with such fervor. Each scene that unfolded on the screen was a stark reminder of the thin line between success and failure in the unforgiving world of show business. The characters they had portrayed, so full of ambition and determination, now appeared as ghostly reminders of their lost potential.

Watching On the Set, Fred and Caleb were forced to confront the reality of their situations. The show, which had once been a symbol of hope, now illuminated the contrast between the bright promise of their early careers and the more challenging realities they faced. The disparity between the characters they had played and the men they had become was laid bare, a juxtaposition that was both illuminating and disheartening.

As the episodes progressed, the initial nostalgia gave way to a deeper introspection. Fred and Caleb were drawn into a reflective state, where the boundaries between their characters' struggles and their personal battles became increasingly blurred. As it is a bizarre experience to watch yourself on television. The gritty realism of the show, once a source of artistic pride, now served as a mirror reflecting their own experiences with fame, addiction, and the quest for redemption. The journey of their characters, so vividly portrayed on screen, resonated with their own lives, a parallel narrative of ambition, loss, and the elusive nature of success.

The viewing of these episodes was not just a trip down memory lane but a confrontation with the choices they had made and the consequences of those choices. It was a reminder that the pursuit of fame and success, so often glamorized, was fraught with challenges and pitfalls. For Fred and Caleb, the experience was a cathartic one, offering them a chance to reflect on their journey, to mourn what might have been, and perhaps to find a sense of closure.

"Look at us, Caleb," Fred murmured, a hint of nostalgia in his voice as he pointed at their younger, more vibrant selves on the screen. "We actually looked alive back then."

Caleb snorted, taking another drag from his cigarette. "Alive...maybe. Naive? Definitely. We thought we had it all figured out, didn't we?"

The scene on the television shifted to one of their most intense moments on the show: a confrontation scene that had been as real as it gets. Fred watched himself on screen, the raw emotion, the anger, and frustration all pouring out in a performance that had felt all too real even then.

"I remember that day," Fred said, his voice barely above a whisper. "I wasn't acting, Caleb. That was me, all my anger, all my pain, right there, on drugs."

Caleb turned to look at him, the flickering light reflecting in his eyes. "I know, man. I felt it too. That's why they wanted us to do this. It was real for both of us. Too real."

"Did you ever think it would end up like this?" Caleb asked, breaking the silence as the credits started to roll.

Fred shook his head, a bitter laugh escaping him. "Never. I thought we were on our way up. That show was supposed to be our big break, not our downfall."

The transition to the behind-the-scenes segment on the television screen brought with it a wave of nostalgia, transporting Fred and Caleb back to a time when the weight of the world seemed lighter on their shoulders. The footage, filled with candid moments of laughter and camaraderie, captured the essence of a period in their lives marked by optimism and a sense of invincibility.

Fred's voice, tinged with a mixture of nostalgia and regret, broke the silence once more. "Look at us, joking around without a care in the world. We didn't know how good we had it," he remarked, his words heavy with the weight of hindsight.

Caleb, too, was deeply affected by the images flickering before them. "We were kings of our little world, Fred. But kingdoms fall, and so did we," he said, his voice imbued with a somber acceptance of their shared fate.

In the silence that followed Caleb's poignant observation, a shared sense of understanding and empathy emerged between the two men. They recognized that their experiences, though marred by loss and regret, were also filled with moments of genuine connection and joy. The behind-the-scenes footage, a visual testament to their former lives, served as a bridge between who they *were and who they had become, highlighting the enduring nature of their friendship and the indomitable spirit of resilience that had carried them through their darkest days. As they sat in the dimly lit room, watching the remnants of their past unfold on the screen, Fred and Caleb were reminded that, despite the trials they had faced, the essence of their bond and the memories of better times remained an integral part of their story, a source of strength in the continuing saga of their lives.*

As the final episode of On the Set concluded, the room was engulfed in a profound silence, a stark contrast to the vibrance onscreen.

Eventually, Fred's voice cut through the silence, tinged with a mixture of desperation and determination. "We can get back there, you know," he asserted, his words infused with a fervent belief in the possibility of redemption. "We can get clean, get back on track. It doesn't have to end like this." His statement was not just an expression of hope but a plea for change, a call to arms against the despair that threatened to engulf them.

Caleb's response to Fred's declaration was a complex mixture of emotions. At first, a glimmer of hope sparked within him, a fleeting sense of possibility that perhaps all was not lost. This initial reaction, however, was quickly overshadowed by a wave of skepticism borne of the many disappointments and challenges they had faced. "Can we, Fred? After everything?" he questioned, his voice heavy with doubt.

The exchange between Fred and Caleb was a crossroads marked by the tension between hope and despair, between the desire for redemption and the fear of further failure. Fred's insistence on the possibility of change, of clawing their way back from the brink, was a tribute to the resilience of the human spirit, to the belief that even in our darkest moments, the potential for transformation exists.

Caleb's skepticism, on the other hand, served as a reminder of the complexities of such a journey, of the doubts and uncertainties that inevitably accompany any attempt to alter the course of one's life.

Fred reached for the remote and turned off the TV, plunging the room into complete darkness. "We have to try, Caleb. It's the only scene we haven't played out yet."

Fred and Caleb reached a tacit understanding, a mutual resolve that transcended words. It was a pact made in the heart of darkness, a vow to embark on a journey fraught with uncertainty and peril, but one that promised the glimmer of redemption. The silence of the room bore witness to this pivotal decision, marking the beginning of an endeavor to recapture the essence of who they once were, to step out of the long shadows cast by their past mistakes and into the light of potential renewal. This uncharted path they committed to tread was strewn with obstacles, each step forward a test of their resolve, their courage, and their willingness to confront the demons that had led them astray.

The realization that the road ahead would be arduous, potentially even more challenging than any role they had ever played, weighed heavily upon them. The specter of failure loomed large; a constant reminder of the risks inherent in attempting to alter the trajectory of lives that had veered so dramatically off course. Yet, the prospect of continuing to exist as mere shadows of their former selves, trapped in a cycle of addiction and regret, was a fate both Fred and Caleb were unwilling to accept. The decision to change, to fight for a future unmarred by the mistakes of the past, was born out of a profound dissatisfaction with their current state and a fervent desire for redemption.

As they sat together in the stillness, a sense of solemnity enveloped them, an awareness that they were on the cusp of the most significant performance of their lives. Unlike the roles they had portrayed on screen, this challenge offered no script, no predetermined outcomes, only the raw reality of their shared human experience. The journey upon which they were about to embark required not the memorization of lines but the mustering of inner strength, the ability to face each day with determination, and the resilience to overcome the inevitable setbacks that lay ahead.

The revelation that both Fred and Caleb had succumbed once again to addiction since the filming of the show added a layer of complexity to their resolve. Their descent back into the throes of dependency served as a poignant reminder of the insidious nature of addiction, its capacity to ensnare and derail even the most promising of lives. This regression into old habits underscored the urgency of their decision to seek change, highlighting the precariousness of their situation and the critical need for action.

In this moment of shared vulnerability and determination, Fred and Caleb found themselves united by a common goal: to break free from the chains of addiction and rebuild their lives from the ground up. The path to recovery they envisioned for themselves was not merely a return to sobriety but a comprehensive transformation, an opportunity to rediscover their purpose, to mend the relationships that had been fractured by their actions, and to carve out a place for themselves in a world that had moved on without them.

As the night wore on, the silent agreement forged between them in the darkness became a beacon of hope, a testament to the human capacity for change and the power of friendship and mutual support. The journey ahead would undoubtedly test their resolve, challenging them to confront the realities of their addiction and the consequences of their choices. Yet, in deciding to try, to embark on this arduous journey together, Fred and Caleb had taken the first, crucial step toward reclaiming their lives.

Chapter 14

TOM PHELPS

Tom Phelps' office was a symbol of the chaotic nature of his profession, with stacks of manuscripts and papers crowding every available surface. Seated amidst this organized disarray, Tom was wholly focused on the call at hand. His critique of the manuscript in question was merciless, delivered with a sharp wit that left little room for ambiguity. "Listen, darling, your manuscript? It's like watching paint dry, but at least paint eventually dries into something nice. Yours just...doesn't," he remarked, the smirk evident in his voice.

The author on the other end of the line was caught off guard by Tom's harsh assessment. "I-I spent years on that novel, Mr. Phelps. I was hoping for some constructive criticism, not..." The author's voice trailed off, a mix of disappointment and disbelief coloring the unfinished protest.

Tom, however, was unyielding, his impatience with what he perceived as the author's naivete apparent in his swift interruption. "Not what? The truth?" he retorted, his eyes rolling in exasperation. Tom's philosophy was uncompromising, rooted in the belief that honesty, no matter how brutal, was a necessary component of the creative process. "Look, if you want sugar-coated lies, go talk to your mom. She'll tell you it's a masterpiece because she has to. Me? I tell it like it is. And 'like it is' means your book's a snoozefest," he declared, his tone leaving no doubt as to his verdict on the manuscript's merits—or lack thereof.

For the hopeful author, Tom's words were a bitter pill to swallow, a jarring confrontation with the possibility that the years of *effort might not culminate in the success they had envisioned. Yet, for Tom, this was another day at the office, another opportunity to wield his brand of truth-telling in service of what he believed to be the greater good of literature. His disdain for mediocrity, for works that failed to stir the soul or challenge the mind, was a driving force behind his interactions with authors, a guiding principle that informed his every critique.*

As the call ended and the silence of the office enveloped him once more, Tom Phelps remained ensconced behind his cluttered desk, a solitary figure in the tumultuous world of publishing. His commitment to honesty, though often perceived as cruelty, was an integral aspect of his identity as a literary agent. In a business saturated with unfulfilled dreams and unrealized potential, Tom stood as a gatekeeper, a fire that illuminates the harsh reality in a sea of hopeful aspirations. The conversation with the author, though just one of many, was a stark reminder of the high stakes involved in the pursuit of literary acclaim, a pursuit that Tom navigated with a mixture of cynicism, humor, and an unwavering belief in the sanctity of truth.

Before the author could reply, Tom's assistant, Sarah, timidly knocked and entered his office. "Mr. Phelps, your ten o'clock is here." Her voice was barely above a whisper.

Tom waved dismissively at the phone. "Gotta run, sweetheart. Maybe try poetry? Shorter, at least." He hung up without waiting for a response and fixed his gaze on Sarah. "Well, let's hope this one's got something less coma-inducing. Who is it?"

Sarah hesitated, her eyes darting to the floor. "It's Jenna Marley, the young adult fiction writer."

"Ah, the vampire romance saga," Tom snorted as he stood up. "Because what the world needs is more lovesick vampires. Send her in, then. Let's get this over with."

Jenna stepped into Tom Phelps' office, her heart racing as she navigated the threshold of opportunity and apprehension. She had prepared for this moment, rehearsing her pitch, bolstering her resolve with the hope that her manuscript would find favor with one of the industry's most notoriously discerning literary agents. Yet no amount of preparation could fully shield her from the bundle of nerves threatening to undermine her carefully curated façade of confidence.

"Mr. Phelps, it's an honor to meet you," she began, her voice laced with respect and anticipation, eager to make a positive impression. "I've heard so much about—"

Tom's cut through Jenna's greeting with the sharpness of a well-practiced wit. "About how I'm the only one in this town with any taste? Yeah, I get that a lot," he quipped. He remained seated, his demeanor casual to the point of indifference, signaling a challenge to Jenna's aspirations before the conversation had truly begun. "So, vampires, huh? What's the twist? They sparkle in the sunlight? Oh, wait. That's been done to death, pardon the pun."

Jenna, undeterred by Tom's brusque reception, summoned her resolve, determined to articulate the unique aspects of her work. She forced a smile, a gesture of diplomacy in the face of his skepticism. "Actually, my story explores deeper themes, like the struggle for identity and the concept of immortality impacting personal growth," she explained.

Tom leaned back, feigning interest. "Deep themes with vampires. Right. Because when I think 'depth,' I definitely think 'bloodsuckers.' Look, Jenna, was it? The vampire train has left the station, crashed, and burned. You want a piece of advice? Ditch the fangs, focus on something original."

Feeling deflated but determined, Jenna pressed on. "I believe there's still an audience for my work. With the right guidance, I can—"

"Guidance?" Tom laughed, loud and harsh. "Sweetheart, what you need isn't guidance; it's a miracle. But hey, miracles happen, right? Just not here. Not with this." He waved a dismissive hand.

Jenna stood up, her resolve hardening. "Thank you for your time, Mr. Phelps. I'll seek representation elsewhere."

As Jenna left, Sarah peeked in, her expression apologetic. "Was that really necessary, Mr. Phelps?"

Tom's demeanor, a blend of nonchalance and cleverness, seemed unshaken. His approach to his professional life was not for the faint of heart.

"What? Telling the truth? Always necessary, Sarah. How else will they learn?" he retorted; his words laced with a conviction that bordered on defiance.

Tom viewed his candor not as a liability but as a necessary tool of his trade, a means to sift through the pretense and get to the heart of matters, even if it meant ruffling feathers along the way.

Sarah, accustomed to Tom's abrasive style yet never fully desensitized to it, offered a resigned sigh. Her voice, soft and measured, contrasted starkly with Tom's brashness. "Lunch with the publishers from Harrison & Co. They're looking forward to discussing the new memoir you're representing." Her tone hinted at a plea for a modicum of diplomacy.

Tom's reaction to the mention of the memoir was predictably disdainful. "Great, another delusional has-been thinking their life stories worth a damn. This day just keeps getting better." Standing up, he straightened his tie with a smug smirk. "Well, let's not keep the delusions waiting. Lead the way, Sarah," he commanded, his tone implying that the upcoming meeting was little more than a necessary evil, a hurdle to be cleared in the pursuit of his professional obligations.

Tom's reputation as a literary agent who refused to sugarcoat his opinions, who wore his disdain for mediocrity like a badge of honor, was both his greatest strength and his most significant liability. His ability to cut through the noise and identify genuinely promising talent was unparalleled, but his methods often left a trail of bruised egos and severed relationships in his wake. Oblivious—or perhaps indifferent—to the bridges he burned, Tom continued on his path, convinced of the righteousness of his approach. For him, the world of literature was not a place for the timid or the insincere; it was an arena where only the truly exceptional deserved to thrive, and he saw himself as the gatekeeper, the arbiter of literary worth in a sea of mediocrity.

As they made their way to the lunch meeting with the publishers from Harrison & Co., Tom and Sarah navigated the complex landscape of the literary world, a universe where ambition, talent, and ego often collide. For Tom, the meeting represented another opportunity to wield his unique brand of honesty, to shape the future of the literary landscape according to his uncompromising standards. For Sarah, it was another day in the life of working with the industry's most controversial figure, a constant balancing act between supporting Tom's vision and mitigating the fallout from his unrelenting candor. Together, they stepped into the unknown, ready to confront whatever challenges and opportunities awaited them, united by a shared commitment to their work, even as they navigated the turbulent waters of Tom's professional ethos.

Chapter 15

CALEB AND MIRABELLE (THEIR FIRST DATE)

The botanical gardens, with their expanse of lush foliage and meticulously maintained flora, served as a verdant stage for the unfolding romance between Mirabelle and Caleb. The crispness of the evening air hinted at the onset of autumn, it's cool touch gently brushing against their skin as they strolled side by side, their steps in sync on the cobblestone path that wound its way through the heart of this natural oasis. The gardens, in their tranquil beauty, seemed to stand apart from the rush and noise of the city beyond its walls, offering a secluded haven where time slowed, allowing for moments of genuine connection and reflection.

Mirabelle, her figure wrapped in the soft embrace of a light shawl, cast occasional glances at Caleb, each look a blend of admiration and curiosity. His calm demeanor and the thoughtful expressions that crossed his face as they talked sparked within her a flutter of anticipation, a feeling that had lain dormant for far too long. Caleb, equally captivated by Mirabelle, found himself drawn not just by her physical presence but by the depth of her insight and the warmth of her laughter. Her stories, rich with the triumphs and trials from her high school years, were shared with a candor and vivacity that Caleb found irresistibly endearing. Each anecdote, each shared memory, seemed to weave a stronger bond between them, a connection that was as unexpected as it was welcome.

Their conversation meandered as freely as their path through the garden, spanning a wide array of topics. They became submerged in discussions about their favorite books and movies, uncovering shared tastes and discovering new ones. Caleb talked about his passion for writing, describing the joy and frustration that came with the creative process, his words painting a vivid picture of his artistic journey. Mirabelle, in turn, spoke of her aspirations, the dreams that propelled her forward, and the challenges that tested her resolve. Throughout their exchange, there was an undercurrent of mutual respect and a growing sense of kinship, as if they were both surprised and delighted by the ease with which they connected.

The garden around them seemed to respond to their burgeoning affinity, with the vibrant hues of flowers under the soft glow of twilight creating a collage of colors that mirrored the complexity and beauty of human emotion. They paused occasionally to admire a particularly striking bloom or to listen to the distant sound of water cascading in a fountain, each shared observation and moment of silence adding layers to their burgeoning relationship.

As the evening deepened, the hours slipped by unnoticed, the passage of time marked only by the changing sky and the subtle shift in the air. Their stroll eventually brought them to a secluded bench near an enchanted fountain, its water reflecting the first stars of the night. Here, they allowed the conversation to come to a natural pause, a comfortable silence settling between them as they contemplated the tranquility of the moment and their unexpected, blossoming intimacy.

It was Mirabelle who finally broke the silence, her voice soft but clear, expressing her gratitude for the evening and the company. Caleb responded in kind, his words reflecting the warmth and affection he felt, a sentiment Mirabelle clearly reciprocated.

It was in this moment that Caleb, driven by a burgeoning sense of connection and affection, reached out to take Mirabelle's hand. The contact was light, hesitant at first, yet charged with an electric current of emotion that surged through them both, a tangible manifestation of the feelings quietly growing between them. For Mirabelle, the sensation of Caleb's hand in hers was a thrill, a leap of faith that sent her heart racing, her skin tingling with the promise of something new.

Upon following the sound of dancing water, they found the enchanting fountain, its soft, melodious murmur creating a backdrop of peaceful contemplation, inviting them to pause and simply be present with one another. The setting sun cast a gentle glow over the scene, bathing everything in a warm, golden light that seemed to ignite the very air around them with a sense of magic and possibility. It was in this moment of tranquil beauty that Caleb, driven by a burgeoning sense of connection and affection, reached out to take Mirabelle's hand. The contact was light, hesitant at first, yet charged with an electric current of emotion that surged through them both, a tangible manifestation of the feelings that had been quietly growing between them. For Mirabelle, the sensation of Caleb's hand in hers was a thrill, a leap of faith that sent her heart racing, her skin tingling with the promise of something new.

The transition from the enchantment of the garden to the warm, inviting atmosphere of the restaurant was seamless, as if the evening was unfolding according to some divine script, each setting perfectly chosen to nurture the delicate bond forming between them. The restaurant, with its cozy ambiance and softly lit interiors, provided a haven from the outside world, a space where time seemed to slow, allowing them to savor each moment, each shared glance, and every whispered conversation. The menu, carefully selected by Caleb to accommodate Mirabelle's vegetarian preferences, was affirmation of his attentiveness and desire to make *the evening as perfect as possible. As they dined, the exchange of stories and laughter flowed as freely as the wine, each course bringing with it new topics of conversation, new opportunities to explore the depths of their personalities and dreams.*

Throughout the meal, there were moments of vulnerability, when the masks of everyday composure were set aside, and the raw, unguarded selves were allowed to surface. These moments, though fleeting, were profound, offering glimpses into the very souls of Mirabelle and Caleb, revealing the fears, hopes, and dreams that lay beneath the surface. Mirabelle, moved by Caleb's openheartedness and the sincere interest he showed in her thoughts and feelings, felt a deepening of the connection that had sparked between them. For Caleb, the experience of being truly seen and heard by Mirabelle was both exhilarating and humbling, a reminder of the beauty of genuine human connection.

As the evening progressed, the conversation meandered through past experiences, future aspirations, and the myriad of small, seemingly inconsequential details that, when shared, serve to weave the intricate menagerie of a budding relationship. With each story, each shared memory, and every burst of laughter, the bond between them grew stronger, more resilient, anchored in a mutual understanding and respect that was both rare and precious.

As the evening's symphony reached its crescendo with the final course of their meal, the ambiance of the restaurant seemed to hold its breath, enveloping Mirabelle, and Caleb in a moment of profound connection. The dessert before them was no longer just a sweet conclusion to their dinner but a shared experience, a symbol of the delightful journey they had embarked on together. Caleb's voice, imbued with a warmth and gentleness that deeply appealed to Mirabelle, broke the silence. "Mirabelle, I feel incredibly lucky to be spending this evening with you. There's something truly special about you, and I..." The hesitation in his voice, a delicate pause filled with unspoken emotions and burgeoning hope, hung in the air, reverence to the depth of feeling that had quietly taken root in his heart.

"Caleb, I feel the same. Tonight, has been wonderful, and getting to know you, really know you, has been a gift." Mirabelle, touched by the raw honesty and vulnerability Caleb displayed, felt a surge of affection and kinship towards him. Her response was instinctive, a natural extension of the bond that had flourished between them throughout the evening. Reaching across the table, her fingers met his in a gesture of comfort and assurance, her touch conveying the empathy and warmth that words could only hint at

By the time the dessert course ended, the initial nerves that had accompanied the start of the evening had given way to a comfortable companionship, a sense of belonging that neither Mirabelle nor Caleb had anticipated but both deeply cherished. The restaurant, with its intimate setting and exquisite cuisine, had become the stage for a dance of emotions, a delicate ballet of give and take that had drawn them ever closer, their spirits entwined in a harmony that reverberated with the promise of future encounters, future moments of shared joy and discovery.

As they stepped out of the restaurant, the cool night air embracing them, Mirabelle and Caleb knew that the evening had been more than just a date; it had been a journey of the heart, a voyage into the realms of affection and understanding that had revealed the profound potential of their connection. The botanical garden, with its serene beauty, and the cozy restaurant, with its warm ambiance, had been the perfect settings for this exploration, each moment a step toward a deeper, more meaningful relationship. In the shared glances, the laughter, and the quiet moments of connection, they had discovered not just each other, but also the possibility of a love that was as beautiful and complex as the garden that had witnessed the beginning of their story.

The evening, which had begun as a simple date, had evolved into a profound encounter, a meeting of minds and hearts that defied the ordinary. Mirabelle and Caleb, through their shared moments of laughter, conversation, and silent understanding, had embarked on a journey that promised not just the discovery of each other but also the exploration of the potential for something truly special. The botanical gardens, with their serene beauty and quiet majesty, had borne witness to the unfolding of a relationship that was as beautiful and intricate as the medley of nature that surrounded them. As they concluded their walk, the promise of future meetings, of continued exploration and deepening connection, lingered in the air, a silent vow to pursue the beautiful possibilities that lay ahead.

The culmination of their walk through the botanical gardens marked a poignant moment, as the impending parting cast a shadow over the wondrous connection Mirabelle and Caleb had nurtured throughout the evening. The garden, with its whispering trees and fragrant blooms, had borne witness to the unfolding of a relationship that, in the span of a few hours, had evolved from tentative introductions to a profound mutual understanding and affection. As they approached the garden's exit, the reality of their separation became imminent, tinged with the melancholy that often accompanies the end of a perfect day. Yet, beneath this transient sadness, there was an undercurrent of hope, a shared anticipation of what was yet to come.

Caleb, feeling the weight of the moment, turned to Mirabelle, his heart caught between the desire to extend the night indefinitely and the understanding that all evenings must come to an end. The moonlight, soft and forgiving, illuminated Mirabelle's features, casting her in an ethereal light that seemed to highlight her innate grace and beauty. "May I see you again?" he asked, his voice carrying the weight of his hopes and the depth of his feelings. The question, simple in its phrasing, was laden with significance, a request for permission to continue exploring the potential of their connection, to see where the journey of their budding relationship could lead.

Mirabelle's response was immediate and heartfelt, her smile a radiant reflection of the joy and promise the evening had brought her. "I would like that very much, Caleb," she said, her words imbued with sincerity and a shared eagerness to discover the depths of their connection. Her affirmation was more than just an acceptance of Caleb's request; it was a declaration of her interest and investment in the potential of their relationship, a mutual recognition of the rare and precious bond that had begun to form between them.

Their farewell, though necessitated by the passage of time, was not a goodbye but a promise of future encounters, of opportunities to deepen their understanding of each other and explore the myriad possibilities that lay ahead. It was a silent vow, unspoken yet powerfully present in the space between them, that they would both cherish and nurture the connection they had discovered. They stood at the threshold of tomorrow, poised on the brink of a journey that promised laughter and discovery, challenges and growth, respect and kindness.

As they parted ways, the essence of the evening lingered, a memory woven from the beauty of their surroundings and the authenticity of their interactions. The botanical gardens, with their tranquil paths and vibrant life, had been the perfect backdrop for the beginning of their story, a setting that mirrored the natural, unfolding progression of their relationship. In the quiet of the night, under the watchful gaze of the stars, Mirabelle and Caleb stepped into their respective futures, hearts full of the promise of what was to come.

Their walk through the gardens had been a journey not just through a physical landscape but through the landscapes of their hearts and minds. They had shared stories and dreams, fears, and hopes, each revelation a step closer to one another. The evening had been a manifestation of the beauty of genuine connection, to the potential for two people to find in each other a kindred spirit, a partner in the exploration of life's vast and varied experiences.

As they moved forward, the anticipation of their next meeting was a beacon, guiding them through the uncertainty of tomorrow with the certainty of their shared affection. The promise of future moments together, of continuing the dialogue they had begun and building upon the foundation they had laid, was a source of comfort and excitement. In the end, Mirabelle and Caleb's parting was not an end but a beginning, the first chapter in a story that promised to be as beautiful and intricate as the garden that had seen the start of their journey toward a tomorrow filled with real, heartfelt moments.

As the fog of the night gently enveloped the departing figure of Mirabelle, a poignant moment unfolded, unseen by her but deeply significant for Caleb. Standing alone, with the soft murmur of the city's nightlife as his backdrop, Caleb found himself at a crossroads, both literally and metaphorically. The evening's events, charged with the promise of new beginnings and the warmth of a connection he had scarcely dared to hope for, had ignited within him a resolve to confront the shadows that lingered in the corners of his life. It was a resolve that took physical form as he reached into the depths of his pocket, his fingers wrapping around a small plastic bag whose contents symbolized the very chains he sought to break.

The bag, filled with white powder, was more than just a substance; it was a remnant of a life Caleb was determined to leave behind—a life marked by moments of weakness, escape, and the false solace found in the fleeting oblivion it offered. The decision to rid himself of it was not made lightly; it was the culmination of a journey marked by struggle and introspection. It was a choice following the dawning realization that the path to true fulfillment lay not in ephemeral highs but in real, tangible moments of connection and growth.

With a motion that was both deliberate and symbolic, Caleb lifted a nearby garbage can lid and opened the plastic bag, allowing each particle to disappear into the darkness, signifying the shedding of a past that no longer controlled his future. This act of discarding the powder was more than just a physical release; it was a vow, a solemn promise to himself and to the future he envisioned with Mirabelle—a future built on authenticity, mutual support, and the shared exploration of life's myriad possibilities.

As the fog continued to swirl and the night stretched out before him, Caleb stood for a moment longer, reflecting on the significance of his actions. The weight of the decision to turn away from a path of escape and towards one of engagement and presence was not lost on him. It was a choice that marked the beginning of a new chapter, one characterized by growth, resilience, and the pursuit of a life defined by meaningful relationships and personal integrity.

The journey ahead would undoubtedly be marked by challenges and moments of doubt, but Caleb's actions on this fog-enshrouded evening had set the foundation for a future where such *challenges could be met with the strength of conviction and the support of those, he held dear. As he finally turned to walk away from the garbage can, leaving behind the vestiges of his old life, Caleb stepped into the night with a renewed sense of purpose, his heart buoyed by the promise of a future shared with Mirabelle, a future where each moment of focus, each decision, and each step forward was a building block in the life they would build together.*

Chapter 16

JACK REYNOLDS (THREE MONTHS POST THE NIGHT WITH MICHAEL)

The neon lights of Los Angeles flickered like distant stars, casting long shadows on the pavement. Once celebrated across these very streets, Jack now meandered through them, a bottle in hand, his steps unsteady. The illustrious movie star, known for his magnetic presence on the silver screen, had descended into a spectacle of drunken disarray.

It was well past midnight, but the city buzzed with energy. Fans and passersby who recognized him would occasionally stop, their excitement quickly turning to dismay as they met not the charismatic idol they admired, but a man lost to his vices, slurring insults at those who dared approach.

"Jack Reynolds! I loved you in Eternal Quest!" a young woman exclaimed; her eyes wide with admiration.

Jack squinted at her, the words echoing in his foggy mind. "Loved? Past tense, sweetheart. What, you don't love me now?" he spat, the venom in his voice dripping with self-loathing and alcohol.

The woman recoiled, her expression morphing from adoration to shock. Muttering an apology, she quickly retreated into the crowd, another fan disillusioned by the harsh reality of her hero's downfall.

As Jack continued his aimless wander, the city's vibrant life seemed to mock him, a cruel reminder of the heights from which he had fallen. The roles had dried up, the accolades had ceased, and now, Jack Reynolds, once the darling of Hollywood, was little more than a cautionary tale—a reminder that his behavior on

Hollywood sets was no longer tolerated.

He stumbled upon his star on the Walk of Fame, his engraved name glaring up at him. A bitter laugh escaped his lips as he slouched down beside it, the irony not lost on him. Here he was, literally on top of his grandest achievement, yet at the lowest point of his life.

"Look at you, Jack. A real star," he mumbled to himself, his words soaked in sarcasm and whiskey. He traced the letters of his name with a finger, the cool, hard surface a stark contrast to the warmth of the limelight he once basked in.

People continued to pass by, some pausing to take pictures. Their voices were a distant hum in Jack's ears, their words blending into a meaningless cacophony. None dared to approach him now, the spectacle too uncomfortable, too real.

As the night wore on, Jack's consciousness began to wane, his body succumbing to the alcohol's numbing embrace. His last thoughts before darkness claimed him were filled with regret and a poignant realization of the loneliness his fame had brought him.

He awoke to the first light of dawn, the city's cacophony replaced by a serene quiet. His body ached, a physical vestige of the night's debauchery, and as he slowly sat up, he caught his reflection in a storefront window. The sight of himself—disheveled, lost, and alone—was a jarring confrontation with the man he had become.

Jack Reynolds, the movie star, had vanished, leaving behind a man who had lost himself to the very fame he had once coveted. As he rose to his feet, steadying himself against the cool morning air, he knew it was time to face the long journey back—not to the heights of stardom, but to the man he had once been, and perhaps could be again.

This chapter of Jack's life closed not with the applause of adoring fans or the flash of cameras, but with the sobering silence of introspection and the daunting prospect of redemption as he raised his hand to call his driver who no longer existed. "I could have been Julius Caesar!"

Chapter 17

TOM AND HARVEY PLUS

The office was filled with the usual hustle, but in Tom Phelps' spacious room, time seemed to slow down as he sat behind his large desk, lost in thought. The myriad of files in front of him remained untouched as he stared into space, contemplating. The silence was eventually broken by his loud call.

"Harvey! Come in here."

Harvey, a partner at the entertainment firm, rushed in, slightly out of breath from the sudden summons. "What is all the screaming about?"

"Harvey, I have a very important job for you."

"Really? What is it? Do you want me to sign someone really important?" Harvey's eyes sparkled with anticipation, imagining the possibilities of a high-profile assignment.

"No, Harvey, what I have for you is very special to me. It would be a huge personal favor."

"What is it?"

Tom sighed, his gaze wandering off as if he were about to share a profound secret. "Well, you see, Harvey, all this talk about movies and books and meetings has me thinking… I mean, what is my legacy, Harvey? Yes, I know, I am the 'top agent,' the guy every author and poet runs to if they want to 'win the game.' I have the money, the success, blah, blah, blah. That's not what I'm asking. I'm asking—how will people see me when I'm gone? What kind of man will I be to my kids? What am I going to hand down to my kids besides bad genes and a borderline obsession with parallel lines?"

Harvey, caught off guard by the depth of the conversation, responded with a puzzled, "What?"

Tom continued, more to himself than to Harvey. "You see, at some point in a man's life, he looks at himself in the mirror and says, 'Is that all I have to give? Have I given enough of myself today?'"

Harvey, trying to lighten the mood, quipped, "I try to not look into mirrors; they freak me out."

Tom glanced at him, momentarily distracted from his existential crisis. "Is it the reflection of your own shortcomings or the reflection of your personal failure?"

"I'm pretty sure it's my receding hairline," Harvey replied with a straight face.

Tom chuckled, the tension in the room dissipating slightly. "Harvey, I'm being serious here. I want to create something lasting, something meaningful. Not just for the world, but for my family. I need your help to make it happen."

Harvey nodded solemnly. "Of course, Tom. Whatever you need, I'm here to help. What's the plan?"

Tom leaned back, a new resolve in his eyes. "I want to start a foundation. One that supports young, aspiring filmmakers and writers who don't have the resources we take for granted. I want to give back, Harvey. And I want you to help me set it up."

Harvey, inspired by Tom's sudden shift from cynical agent to philanthropist, stood taller. "That sounds incredible, Tom. Count me in. Where do we start?"

With a renewed sense of purpose, Tom began outlining his vision for the foundation, the two of them brainstorming into the early hours of the morning. For the first time in a long time, Tom Phelps felt like he was working towards a legacy that meant more than just deals and contracts—a legacy of giving back and making a difference. And for Harvey, the reflection in the mirror suddenly didn't seem so daunting anymore.

In the spacious, yet somehow claustrophobic office of Tom Phelps, the air was thick with the kind of tension that only years of working closely together can create. Harvey stood before Tom, his expression a mix of resignation and exasperation, accustomed to the eccentricities of his boss but not entirely immune.

"Aren't you supposed to be an agent? You should probably take care of that," Tom remarked nonchalantly, flipping through some documents on his desk without looking up.

"I will, I will. It's just hard to get an appointment, and I'm not sure that surgery is right for me..." Harvey's voice trailed off, hoping for a semblance of empathy, or at least understanding.

Tom paused, laying down the papers and finally fixing his gaze on Harvey. "Silence." He paused dramatically, ensuring he had Harvey's full attention. "Harvey, this moment we are having here—I have to be honest. I want to hear more about me and less about you."

"So...like every conversation we've ever had?" Harvey shot back, a hint of defiance in his tone.

"More or less."

"More not less."

"Yes."

"You have been saying that."

Tom leaned forward, a serious look on his face. "Harvey, I want to share my life story with you."

"I feel like I have to vomit now," Harvey blurted out.

"What?"

"I get really nauseous when I get anxious," Harvey explained, hoping to deflect the conversation.

"Now don't make me regret telling you this."

"Why would you regret it?"

"I'm telling you, Harvey, I want to share my life story with you."

"Why?"

"You shouldn't be asking 'why?'"

"You do realize that I am a partner and that is more of a secretary's job, right?"

"That's why it's so special. Plus, you're only a junior partner, and I've seen you sort through garbage. I mean, really, Harvey, that's not your job."

"I was looking for my retainer." A flush of embarrassment colored Harvey's cheeks at the memory.

In the spacious yet distinctly personalized office of Tom Phelps, the atmosphere was thick with the peculiar blend of tension and camaraderie that characterized his relationship with Harvey. The exchange between them was as rapid and sharp as ever, a verbal dance they had perfected over time.

"Harvey, you are well into your thirties. You should not have a retainer," Tom remarked, his tone a mix of incredulity and amusement as he leaned back in his chair, eyeing Harvey with a critical gaze.

"Sometimes my teeth feel like they are crowding each other, and it makes me feel self-conscious."

"You would think that that hairline would make you feel more self-conscious."

"Well, I have tried to change shampoos, but they never..." Harvey began, his explanation trailing off as he realized the futility of discussing his haircare routine with Tom.

"Harvey, remember this is about me now."

"Of course, you were going to share your life story with me."

"I was, but now I'm feeling a bit indifferent to the entire thing."

"You were so excited a minute ago."

"Now I'm less excited about it and more concerned with your overall attitude about it."

"You called me in here, and I came running as if there was a fire. But I don't see a fire."

"What if there was a fire? Would you have saved me?" Tom asked, his question hanging between them, weighted with implications beyond their immediate conversation.

"Only because I would want to protect the firm."

"Ha, so you are concerned for my well-being."

"I am a partner and all."

"Junior partner. You have a blue badge; I have an orange badge," Tom reminded him.

"You keep mentioning that, but I think the blue badge looks better."

"Harvey, remember, this is not about you."

"It does match my tie," Harvey concluded, glancing down at his attire, a small victory in their ongoing banter.

Tom leaned back in his oversized office chair, a look of nostalgia washing over his face as he recounted the early days of his career. "So, when I signed my first client, I was twenty-three or twenty-four. I remember that Clinton was president, and I watched a lot of those debates with my girlfriend, Kate. Kate was a wild woman; she always spoke with her lips and not her mouth, which made me...Are you not writing this down?"

Harvey, now sitting across from Tom with a bemused expression, replied, "I am a partner."

"Harvey, these are valuable lessons you can learn. I am talking about sharing experiences with you that I have not even shared with my therapist."

"You have a therapist?"

"I call her Miss Rose, although her name is Violet or Shannon, something exotic. We talk about my travels throughout the Amazon."

"You never go on vacation, though."

"It's Freudian therapy; very dream orientated."

"You talk to your therapist about your dreams?"

"I dream a lot. I am a man not bound by earthly possessions or the lands that surround me. I am a restless soul who constantly seeks out new adventure, either imaginary or not."

"I would open your book with that. 'Either imaginary or not,'" Harvey suggested, finally seeing a glimmer of interest in Tom's narrative.

"You can't open a book like that; you have to use happy words like 'In the beginning' or 'Once upon a time.' Yes, that is how we will begin my story. In the beginning, there was time and space and the agency of Phelps, Anderson, Jenkins, and Kline."

"That is an awful way to start a book."

"What do you know? Plus, I still don't see you writing anything down."

"Maybe you should think about what you want to write about and then call me back in your office."

"Now that is a good way to start the book. It starts with me calling you into my office to start writing, and then it morphs into the story of me walking in on my sister with her boyfriend."

"And why would that be interesting to a reader?"

"Because what they were doing is illegal in ten states,"

"Wow," was all Harvey could say, taken aback by the unexpected twist in Tom's story.

The conversation paused as Caleb entered the room. Tom's earlier jest about being a judge and Harvey's defense of his skincare routine faded into the background as they stood from their chairs, looking at Caleb with expressions of curiosity and concern.

"Caleb, how wonderful it is to see you," Tom greeted, trying to maintain the veneer of professionalism and warmth. "You know, we were just talking about you. How your career is really taking off again," he continued, attempting to steer the conversation toward a more positive light.

"You know he probably doesn't want to discuss all of that right now. I mean, do you, Caleb?" Harvey interjected, his sense of timing impeccable as always, trying to spare Caleb the discomfort of Tom's bluntness.

"No, not really," Caleb replied.

"So, what's on your mind?" Tom asked.

"Well, you know how I've always held you in the highest esteem, right?" Caleb started, his tone earnest, signaling the importance of what he was about to share.

"I would hope that at this point, you could at least call me friend," Tom responded, his attempt at lightening the mood falling somewhat flat in the face of Caleb's seriousness.

"Tom, I have known you my entire career," Caleb stated, a simple fact that underscored the depth of their relationship, beyond mere business acquaintances.

"That's not really saying that you like him at all, though," Harvey couldn't resist commenting, ever the voice of candor in the room.

"Harvey, let him speak," Tom chided gently.

"I just wanted to tell you before it got out in the tabloids," Caleb said, his voice lowering, hinting at the personal nature of his revelation.

"Wait...Have you been using again?" Harvey asked, his question cutting through the tension.

"Harvey," Tom said sharply, a reprimand for what he deemed an inappropriate question at the moment, though his face betrayed his own concern.

"I know you're wondering too," Harvey defended softly, his gaze fixed on Caleb, awaiting his response.

"So, I think I met someone," Caleb finally revealed, his announcement taking both Tom and Harvey by surprise, not at all what they had braced themselves for.

The conversation in Tom's office had veered into unexpectedly personal territory, the kind that lingered in the air long after the words had been spoken. Caleb's announcement had opened a floodgate of opinions, each reflecting the individual's perspective on life and love.

"Oh, that is great news!" Harvey exclaimed.

"Wait, why are you concerned with meeting someone?" Tom's brow furrowed.

"I'm not. It just happened," Caleb replied.

"Well, why did you let it happen?" Tom pressed, as if Caleb had made a strategic error.

"I don't think you can control that kind of thing," Harvey interjected, trying to impart a bit of wisdom into the conversation.

"You can control everything; it takes total commitment though," Tom countered.

"He is not talking about a job; he is talking about love," Harvey clarified.

"Wait, do you love this girl?" Tom asked.

"It is a little early to think about it in those terms," Caleb admitted, cautious yet optimistic about where this new relationship might lead.

"How is it going to affect your work?" Tom queried.

"Oh, I don't think it will," Harvey replied, hopeful that Caleb's personal happiness wouldn't come at the expense of his professional success.

"Who asked you?" Tom snapped, his patience thinning, not ready to concede Harvey's point.

"No one, but that never stopped me before. I think it is going to change his life in a good way," Harvey said.

"I have seen too many people walk through those doors and tell me that their world is changing. That change has ruined them," Tom revealed.

"Why did it ruin them?" Harvey asked.

"It's the way the world works. You are successful; why would you want it to change?" Tom responded.

"I'm not really that successful," Caleb admitted, a hint of resignation in his voice. His recent strides in life were overshadowed by his struggles, making his achievements feel diminished.

"That is because you keep trying to change things," Tom retorted.

"I am excited for him; meeting someone to care about is important."

"Making money is more important," Tom countered.

"Not as important as an intimate connection to another human being," Harvey argued.

"No one needs that," Tom dismissed, his stance firm, reflecting a lifetime of prioritizing career over personal connections.

"I do," Caleb said simply.

"I just have some concerns, Caleb. I mean, it's only been six months since you got out of rehab. The wounds are still fresh," Tom voiced his worries, not as a dismissal of Caleb's feelings but as a guardian of his well-being, albeit in his characteristically blunt manner.

"Tom, you know I really don't have family to tell. I want you to at least pretend you're happy about this," Caleb implored.

"I am happy for you, but I have some concerns. Any mental health professional would tell you that a year just isn't enough time. Plus, you have a career to worry about," Tom reasoned, his concern laced with a caution that bordered on pessimism.

"Tom, I have thought about this and decided it's right," Caleb asserted, his determination shining through the cloud of doubt Tom was casting.

"How much thinking did you really do?" Tom questioned.

"I filled three journals worth," Caleb revealed.

"But was it that sad 9th-grade poetry kind of writing?" Tom joked, trying to lighten the mood but also probing the sincerity and maturity of Caleb's reflections.

"Come on, Tom, I'm serious," Caleb insisted.

"I am too, with the hearts and doodles," Tom quipped, unwilling to let the moment pass without injecting his brand of humor, even at the risk of belittling Caleb's earnestness.

"There were a few doodles," Caleb conceded, a small smile breaking through his earlier annoyance, acknowledging the absurdity of their back-and-forth.

"Well, I'm happy to hear this news," Harvey finally said, bringing the conversation back to its heartening core.

"Nobody cares if you're happy or not; you're a junior partner. The only reason you're on the stationary is because your father bought your way in," Tom said sharply to Harvey.

"That is not...okay, it is true...but, I—" Harvey stammered.

"Have a receding hairline," Tom continued, relentless in his critique.

"I just wanted to tell you about it and see if it meant anything to you," Caleb interjected, seeking some semblance of support, or understanding.

"That is a little soon, don't you think?" Tom questioned.

"You see, that is what is great about it; I am just so caught up in love that I don't think about time anymore," Caleb explained, his voice filled with a passion that seemed alien to the room's current atmosphere.

"Is that why we aren't getting pages from you?" Tom asked, his concern for Caleb's career momentarily overshadowing the personal revelation.

"I just handed in 400 pages for my next novel," Caleb defended.

"Is it called 'I love 'random girl's name''?" Tom quipped, unable to resist a jab at what he perceived as Caleb's infatuation-driven distraction.

"Her name is Mirabelle," Caleb said firmly, not willing to let Tom's cynicism taint his feelings.

"Where do I know that name from?" Tom mused.

"Sounds like a waitress name," Harvey commented, remembering the woman from their frequent bar visits.

"Yes, she was the waitress at the bar," Tom recalled.

"She isn't a waitress; she is a cocktail waitress," Caleb corrected, emphasizing the distinction as if it added a layer of respectability to Mirabelle's profession.

"That one extra word makes it all better," Tom replied sarcastically.

"Sometimes the simplest words can make it seem classier," Caleb argued.

"Caleb, you can't spend time with a waitress. You are a successful writer, and you have this movie and that TV show you were on. On the Set is the number one show in America right now! People love your struggle!" Tom proclaims.

"She's great, and I have dated actresses before; they have nothing to say," Caleb countered.

"Then change the conversation to something they're interested in," Tom suggested.

"I have no idea what they would be interested in," Caleb admitted.

"Have you tried talking to them about anorexia or bulimia?" Tom asked, his question crossing the line from insensitivity into outright offensiveness.

Harvey, leaning against the wall with a smirk, had just shared his idea for marketing Caleb's new book when Tom's skepticism cut through the air.

"T-shirts? Really?" Tom questioned.

"I think in design, and you think in people. That is why I have more Facebook friends than you," Harvey retorted, quick to defend his idea and poke fun at Tom's expense simultaneously.

Caleb, caught in the middle of this exchange, couldn't help but reflect on the turn the conversation had taken. "This played out completely differently in my head."

"It always does," Tom replied.

As the conversation waned, Tom found himself quietly inspired by the exchange. "I think I just thought of a second chapter for my book," he mused aloud, his earlier irritation giving way to a spark of creativity fueled, in part, by the very interactions he often critiqued.

"I'm still not going to write it down," Harvey quipped.

"So, what's your new book called?" Tom asked, turning his attention back to Caleb, perhaps seeking to redirect the conversation to a safer, less contentious topic.

"The Greatest Empire Ever Sold," Caleb announced, his voice steady, the title of his new project imbued with the kind of ambition and mystery that had first drawn Tom to him as a client.

"I like that name. It's catchy. Little T-shirts with little plots of *land on them,"* Harvey chimed in, unable to resist another dig at Tom's expense, envisioning a marketing strategy that blended Caleb's literary aspirations with his own design sensibilities.

Chapter 18

FRED WILLIAMS – THE SILHOUETTE

Fred Williams, whose life had once been as brightly lit as the hot microphone he once performed with, found himself in a period of profound introspection and transformation. The contrast between the man he had become and the character he portrayed on the critically acclaimed television show On the Set was stark and filled with irony. Fred's character, a drug addict entangled in the grip of his demons, earned him accolades and recognition, yet it was this very portrayal that seemed to foreshadow his spiraling descent into a similar abyss. The shadows of his past choices and the role that had re-established his career on the radio now served as a constant reminder of the dualities of his existence: the public persona celebrated for his talent and the private individual struggling to find his way out of the darkness.

Fred's living room, a modest and somewhat disorganized space, had become the center stage for his journey of redemption. Amid the clutter and the dim glow cast by the television screen, Fred sought solace and a sense of purpose. The room, with its tangible reminders of both his past successes and present struggles, was a microcosm of his life's current state: a blend of memories, aspirations, and the harsh realities of attempting to change. On the Set, with its dramatic narratives and complex characters, played in the background, serving as a mirror to Fred's own tumult and metamorphosis. The show, once a source of embarrassment and professional pride, had transformed into a cathartic element in his daily life, a way to face his own story with a blend of critical detachment and personal investment.

Fred's daily engagement with On the Set had transformed into a cornerstone of his routine, a ritual that served multiple purposes in his life. It was a bridge to his past, a stark reminder of the divergent paths between the character he portrayed and the man he had become. Watching the show, Fred was transported back to a time when his career was on the ascent, when each episode filmed felt like a steppingstone toward greater acclaim and professional fulfillment. The familiarity of the scenes and dialogue, once cues for performance, now prompted Fred to reflect on the arc of his life both in and out of the spotlight.

This process of reflection was not without its challenges. Each episode of On the Set held a mirror to Fred's own life as an addict, showing him an image of himself and his struggles with addiction. The irony that he, who had so convincingly portrayed a man ensnared by drugs, had himself succumbed to similar demons was not lost on Fred. Although this was his thought process and not reality. It was he who portrayed the character without a façade. This realization pierced through the nostalgia, offering a sobering reminder of the fine line between art imitating life and life imitating art. It highlighted the unpredictability of existence, where the roles we play can sometimes foreshadow or even shape our realities.

Yet, amidst the pain of these realizations, Fred found a glimmer of hope. The ritual of watching the show became a form of catharsis, a means of grappling with his past choices and their consequences. It allowed him to confront the darkest parts of his psyche, to acknowledge the mistakes and missteps that had led him to this moment of solitude and self-examination. This confrontation was not merely an exercise in self-pity but a deliberate act of self-discovery, a step toward understanding the depth of his struggles and the potential for transformation.

Fred's resolve to change his narrative was fueled by a complex mixture of emotions. Regret played a significant role, as he mourned the lost opportunities and the damage inflicted on relationships once held dear. The recognition of what could have been, had his choices been different, had he stayed sober, weighed heavily on him, a burden of what-ifs that could easily have mired him in despair. Yet, it was this very regret that also propelled him forward, a catalyst for the determination to forge a new path, to piece together the fragments of his life into a coherent whole.

This determination was rooted in a growing sense of self-worth, a belief in his ability to rise above the challenges that had plagued him. Fred's ritual of watching On the Set evolved into a commemoration of his resilience, a daily reaffirmation of his commitment to change. The show, once a reminder of a life spiraling out of control, now served as a source of strength and inspiration. It reminded Fred that change, while fraught with difficulty and uncertainty, was within his grasp. That drugs didn't have to rule his world. Each episode watched, each moment of reflection endured, was a step toward reclaiming the dignity and sense of purpose that addiction had stripped away.

In the solitude of his living room, surrounded by the vestiges of his former glory, Fred embarked on a journey of redemption. It was a journey marked by solitude, reflection, and the slow, painstaking process of rebuilding. On the Set served as both a companion and a guide, a narrative that paralleled his own but also offered a roadmap for recovery. Through this ritual, Fred engaged in a dialogue with himself, confronting the realities of his situation while also envisioning a future where the mistakes of the past were lessons learned, not chains that bound him.

As Fred wrestled with his emotions and the realities of his journey, the show became a shining example of possibility, illuminating the path towards a life defined not by the shadows of addiction but by the light of self-awareness and growth. In the quiet of his living room, with the television flickering, Fred Williams found himself at the precipice of change, ready to step into the uncertainty of redemption with a resolve forged from the very depths of his struggles.

In the solitude of his living room, a space marked by the remnants of a life once lived in the glaring spotlight, Fred Williams found himself at a crossroads. The television show On the Set, a narrative that had once been a source of pride and professional fulfillment, had morphed into a poignant reflection of his own personal journey. Each episode, with its portrayal of struggle and redemption, mirrored Fred's own battle with the demons that had led him from fame to obscurity.

As Fred watched the drama unfold on screen, his living room transformed into a haven of introspection and self-renewal. The clutter and dim lighting, rather than symbols of neglect, became the backdrop against which his fight for redemption was cast. It was here, amid the echoes of his character's fictional struggles, that Fred embarked on a journey of profound self-discovery. Each day presented a new opportunity to confront the choices that had led him to this moment, to sift through the wreckage of the past in search of the promise of a brighter future.

The ritual of watching On the Set evolved into a crucial component of Fred's quest for redemption. The show, with its narratives of conflict and resolution, offered Fred a mirror through which he could view his own life from a distance, allowing him to engage with his experiences from a new perspective. This daily engagement with the show became a form of therapy, a way for Fred to process his emotions and chart a course toward recovery. The struggles of his on-screen character, once merely scripts to be acted out, now resonated with Fred on a deeply personal level, serving as a stark reminder of his own battles and the possibility of overcoming them.

In his lived-in sanctuary, determination and despair waged a silent war. Fred's resolve to reclaim his life from the clutches of addiction was tested daily by the weight of regret and the lure of escape. Yet, it was within this very struggle that Fred found the seeds of hope for a future unburdened by the past. His once-promising career, though now a shadow of its former self, provided a foundation upon which he could rebuild. The memories of accolades and applause, rather than serving as painful reminders of what had been lost, became sparks of motivation, reigniting his yearning to achieve the redemption he so desperately sought.

Fred's journey of self-awareness and renewal was marked by small, incremental steps. Each episode of On the Set watched, each moment in the solitude of his living room, contributed to a growing sense of personal resilience. The show, once a symbol of his professional achievements, now played a pivotal role in his personal recovery, offering Fred a narrative framework within which he could understand and confront his own story.

This daily ritual, set against the backdrop of On the Set, allowed Fred to navigate the complexities of his emotions and to envision a path forward. The living room, cluttered and dimly lit, became a crucible for transformation, a place where the vestiges of a shattered career and the challenges of addiction were met with a steadfast commitment to change. Amid the fictional dramas playing out on the screen, Fred's real-life battle for redemption unfolded, a tribute to the power of resilience and the enduring hope for a second chance.

As Fred Williams sat in the fading light of his living room, the drama of On the Set serving as both a mirror and a guide, he embarked on a path of healing and self-renewal. In this space, where determination confronted despair, Fred found the courage to face his demons, to sift through the detritus of the past, to plant the seeds for a future reclaimed from the shadows of addiction. It was a journey fraught with challenges, but one that held the promise of redemption and the rediscovery of a life once thought lost.

Fred Williams' daily engagement with On the Set evolved into more than just a passive viewing experience; it became a profound journey into the essence of storytelling and its impact on the human spirit. As the episodes unfolded in the quiet of his living room, Fred was constantly reminded of how closely art parallels life, and vice versa. The struggles and triumphs of the characters onscreen deeply affected him, blurring the lines between the fictional world and his reality. This connection served as a powerful reminder of the universal themes of struggle, redemption, and the possibility of change that are intrinsic to both the stories we tell and the lives we lead.

In this intimate setting, where the glow of the television screen often provided the only illumination, Fred found himself reflecting on his own narrative. The show, with its compelling portrayal of human complexity and resilience, offered him a lens through which to examine his past decisions, his present circumstances, and his aspirations for the future. It was a stark reminder of the role choices play in shaping our destinies, and the capacity for renewal that lies within each of us. For Fred, once a celebrated figure in the world of entertainment, the show became a motivating force, challenging him to confront his life with honesty and courage.

This introspective journey was punctuated each morning by a tangible commitment to change. Fred's living room, which doubled as his personal gym, housed the modest workout equipment that had become central to his quest for redemption. Each workout session was an act of defiance against the inertia that had characterized his descent into despair, a physical manifestation of his desire to forge a new path for himself.

One morning, Fred approached his workout with a sense of purpose that felt almost palpable. The determination that fueled him was born out of the recognition that he stood at a critical juncture in his life. With each stride on the treadmill and each lift of the weights, Fred was not just rebuilding his physical strength; he was also working to reconstruct his sense of self-worth and identity. The physical exertion, challenging as it was, paled in comparison to the internal struggle he faced. Yet, it was through this struggle that Fred began to see glimmers of the man he hoped to become— a man defined not by his past failures but by his present efforts and future achievements.

The ritual of his morning workouts, coupled with the reflective moments spent in the company of On the Set, created a rhythm to Fred's days that was both grounding and transformative. The show, with its narrative arcs of downfall and redemption, served as a constant reminder of the possibility of change, inspiring Fred to persevere in his journey toward self-improvement. In this process of daily renewal, Fred found a semblance of peace amid the tumult of his internal landscape. The ongoing struggle to redefine his life and legacy took on a new meaning, infused with a sense of hope and purpose that had long been absent from his life.

Fred's engagement with the fictional world of On the Set and his commitment to physical and emotional health were intertwined threads in the tapestry of his recovery. Each morning brought with it a renewed promise to strive for a better future, to challenge the narratives of despair that had once seemed inescapable. In the stillness of his living room, with the echoes of his character's struggles mingling with his own, Fred Williams embarked on a profound journey of redemption. It was a journey marked by small victories and significant challenges, but above all, it was characterized by Fred's unwavering determination to reclaim his life from the shadows of addiction and to rediscover the joy and fulfillment that come from authentic self-expression and meaningful change.

As Fred Williams embarked on his grueling workout, the effort was both a physical and emotional catharsis. Sweat streamed down his forehead, a visible display of the intensity of his exertion, as he sought to reclaim his body and spirit from the ravages of time and personal turmoil. The steady cadence of his footsteps on the treadmill filled the room, a rhythmic anchor that grounded him in the moment, even as his mind wandered the corridors of his past. Each labored breath he drew was a harsh reminder of the neglect he had subjected himself to, a neglect that had exacted a heavy toll not just on his physical health but on his emotional well-being.

The television screen flickered with scenes from On the Set, the show that had once catapulted him to fame but now served as a poignant mirror reflecting the duality of his existence. As he watched, Fred was struck by the eerie parallels between his life and that of his character. The drama unfolding on screen blurred the lines between fiction and reality, serving as a powerful reminder of the complexities of life, where the roles we play can sometimes become indistinguishable from the lives we lead. Each episode, with its scripted challenges and resolutions, resonated deeply with Fred, evoking a blend of emotions that ranged from nostalgia for his former glory to a profound sense of loss for what might have been.

Yet, amidst the physical strain and the flood of memories, there was an undeniable spark of determination in Fred's eyes. It was the flame of an unyielding will to challenge the narrative of decline that had come to define his life. This resolve was fueled not just *by a desire to regain his physical health but by a deeper longing to rewrite his story, to transform the narrative of downfall into one of redemption and hope.*

As the minutes on the treadmill turned into hours, Fred's journey oscillated between reflections on his past and aspirations for his future. The sharp sting of regret for opportunities missed and relationships damaged was tempered by a growing sense of optimism. On the Set, with its dramatic portrayal of human frailty and resilience, became a source of inspiration, a reminder that, much like the characters he portrayed, he too could confront his demons and emerge stronger.

The show, which had once been a highlight of his acting career, now assumed a new role in Fred's life. It became a catalyst for introspection and a beacon of hope, illuminating the path toward personal redemption. Each scene that played out on the screen, each line delivered by the character he had once brought to life, underscored the universal struggle for meaning and the possibility of renewal. This duality of reflecting on the past while striving for a better future encapsulated Fred's current state—a man caught between the world of his past achievements and the reality of his present struggles, yet determined to forge a path toward a brighter, more fulfilling future.

In this solitary pursuit of redemption, the living room, with its juxtaposition of the flickering television screen and the relentless motion of the treadmill, became a sacred space for transformation. Here, amid the dripping of perspiration and the solitude, Fred Williams found himself engaged in a profound battle against the inertia of despair. It was a fight not just for physical fitness but for the essence of who he was and who he hoped to become. The scenes from On the Set that played in the background of his workout were no longer just remnants of a bygone era but signposts in his journey toward reclaiming his identity and redefining his legacy beyond the confines of the screen.

As Fred Williams pushed the boundaries of his physical endurance, the intensity of his workout escalated to levels he had never before attempted. Each step, each lift, paid homage to his unwavering resolve, a clear signal of his refusal to succumb to the demons of his past. The sweat that drenched his body was not just a sign of physical exertion but a symbol of his deep-seated desire for transformation. Fred was not merely exercising; he was on a quest for redemption, driven by an inner conviction that he could redefine his narrative, that his life need not be a cautionary tale defined by past failures and missed opportunities.

The cluttered room, with its modest array of workout equipment and the flickering glow of the television, became a crucible for Fred's rebirth. The voices from On the Set, once a stark reminder of his former life, now merged into the background, their significance overshadowed by the immediacy of Fred's struggle. His entire being was consumed by the effort, his focus so intense that the external world ceased to exist. The only realities were the burning in his muscles, the relentless pounding of his heart, and the singular determination that propelled him forward.

However, as the journey of On the Set concluded on the screen, a dramatic and unforeseen climax unfolded in Fred's personal narrative. An ominous sensation tightened its grip around his chest, a harbinger of the dire turn his quest for redemption was about to take. The pain, sharp and merciless, bore down on him with a ferocity that left him powerless, forcing him to his knees in a moment of devastating vulnerability. In those harrowing seconds, as the specter of a heart attack loomed large, Fred's tumultuous journey flashed before his eyes, a vivid montage of his life's treasured moments. He attempted to focus on lost loves and connected friendships.

This retrospective was more than a mere recollection of past events; it was an emotional odyssey that traversed the spectrum of human experience. The memories of standing in the spotlight, basking in the adulation of audiences and the acclaim of critics, were juxtaposed with the solitude and despair that had characterized his fall from grace. Fred's life, once defined by the roles he played and the applause he received, now confronted its most profound and final scene in isolation.

The realization that he was experiencing acute pain was accompanied by an awareness of the solitary nature of his battle. Despite the crowded rooms and standing ovations that had once defined his existence, Fred faced this ultimate challenge alone, a stark reminder of the intrinsic loneliness of personal struggles. The journey from celebrity to obscurity, from vitality to vulnerability, had culminated in this moment of existential reckoning.

In the finality of those moments, Fred grappled with the complexity of his legacy, the dichotomy of a life spent in the limelight and the shadows. The sharp, unrelenting pain that enveloped him was not just a physical affliction but a metaphor for the myriad challenges he had faced. His struggle, though deeply personal, echoed the universal themes of human frailty and the search for meaning in the face of adversity.

As Fred succumbed to the overwhelming force of the heart attack, the room that had witnessed his relentless pursuit of change bore silent testimony to the end of his journey. The flickering images of On the Set, the scattered workout equipment, and the dimly lit space were the final witnesses to a life that had oscillated between triumph and tragedy, between the pursuit of redemption and the ultimate surrender to fate. Fred's story, marked by a relentless quest for self-improvement and a tragic conclusion, serves as a poignant reminder of the fragility of life and the enduring quest for meaning amidst the unpredictable vicissitudes of existence.

Fred Williams' life story, a narrative rich with the highs of acclaim and the lows of personal battles, culminated in a moment that was as profound as it was poignant. The silent credits rolling on the television screen marked not just the end of an episode but the closing of a chapter in Fred's life, one that had been fraught with challenges and marked by a relentless pursuit of personal redemption. The room, once filled with the sounds of his determined efforts to regain control over his destiny, now lay in silence, a stark reminder of the suddenness with which life can draw to a close.

Chapter 19

A FAREWELL TO REMEMBER

Caleb Garcia stood firmly at the lectern, his gaze sweeping across the sea of faces before him—friends, family, colleagues, all united in grief and remembrance. The chapel, bathed in the soft light of the afternoon sun, echoed with the weight of the moment. As Caleb inhaled deeply, steadying his nerves, the surrounding quiet seemed to embrace him, offering a moment of peace before he broke the silence.

"Ladies and gentlemen," Caleb began, his voice steady yet filled with emotion. "Today, we find ourselves at a crossroads of sorrow and celebration. We are here to bid farewell to a man whose life was a beacon of hope, friendship, and unwavering spirit—Fred Williams. Fred was more than just a friend to many of us; he was a cherished brother, a guiding mentor, and, in many ways, the anchor that held us steady through the stormiest of seas.

"Fred's journey through life was marked by an insatiable curiosity, a boundless energy for adventure, and an innate ability to see the good in everyone he met. He possessed a rare talent for bringing people together, for forging connections in the unlikeliest of places, and for creating a sense of family wherever he went. His laughter was contagious, his smile radiated warmth, and his generosity knew no bounds.

"But Fred was also a man of profound wisdom and depth. He had an unparalleled ability to listen, to offer counsel that cut through the noise, to speak to the heart of the matter. In my own life, Fred was the lighthouse guiding me back to shore time and *again, his advice a compass by which I navigated the choppy waters of life's challenges.*

"Today, as we gather to mourn his loss, we also come together to celebrate the extraordinary life Fred lived. We celebrate the moments of joy he brought into our lives, the lessons he taught us through his actions and his words, and the indelible marks he left on our hearts. Fred's legacy is not one of material possessions or accolades but of the lives he touched, the people he inspired, and the love he shared freely and without expectation.

"In remembering Fred, we are reminded of the beauty of life, the strength of true friendship, and the power of compassion. He lived his life fully, embracing each day with zest and zeal, pursuing his passions with determination, and always, always putting his loved ones first."

As Caleb spoke, he recognized that most of his statements were only half-truths.

"As we say goodbye to Fred today, let us hold on to the memories we shared, the laughter, the conversations, the quiet moments of understanding. Let us carry forward his spirit of kindness, his unwavering positivity, and his deep-seated belief in the goodness of people. Let us honor his memory by living our lives a little more like Fred did—with open hearts, boundless generosity, and a steadfast commitment to making the world a better place, one act of kindness at a time.

"Fred, my dear friend, your absence leaves a void that cannot be filled, a silence too profound for words. But in our hearts, you remain alive, a guiding star in the night sky, leading us forward. Your legacy will continue to inspire us, to challenge us, and to remind us of the preciousness of life. We will miss you more than words can express, but we are grateful, so profoundly grateful, for the time we had with you, for the love you shared, and for the light you brought into our lives.

"Rest in peace, beloved friend. Your journey here may have ended, but your story lives on through us. We will carry your memory in our hearts always, cherishing the moments we shared and striving to embody the values you lived by. Farewell, Fred, until we meet again."

As Caleb concluded, his voice imbued with a mixture of sorrow and gratitude, the chapel was filled with a palpable sense of loss, but also with a quiet strength—a collective resolve to honor Fred's memory by living as he did, with love, joy, and purpose. The mourners, though tears streamed down many faces, seemed uplifted by Caleb's words, comforted by the reminder of Fred's lasting impact on their lives. In that moment, Fred's spirit seemed to embrace them all, a reminder that though he was gone, his legacy would forever endure.

In the days and weeks that followed, the essence of Caleb's tribute to Fred would linger in the hearts and minds of those who heard it. The symphony of memories and lessons would not only serve as a source of comfort in their grief but as a catalyst for positive change. Inspired by Fred's life, each person would carry a piece of his spirit, ensuring that his legacy of kindness, joy, and unwavering positivity would continue to influence the world in myriad ways, both big and small. The impact of Fred's life would thus become a lasting tribute to the power of love, the strength of community, and the enduring nature of the human spirit.

Chapter 20

LIFE AS WE KNOW IT (TWO YEARS LATER)

In the cozy living room of Mirabelle's house, the air is thick with the silent anticipation of the evening ahead. Caleb, dressed sharply in a suit, stands before a rack holding a collection of ties, each telling a story of past celebrations and moments of decision. He contemplates three or four ties, each a different shade and pattern, weighing their aesthetic merits and considering their compatibility with his suit.

Mirabelle, elegant and poised, gazes into a mirror, her reflection capturing her own moment of contemplation as she applies her makeup with practiced grace. Her expression transitions from a smile to a frown and back, an unspoken narrative of her thoughts and emotions playing across her face. She wears a dress that speaks of elegance and an understanding of the occasion's significance, her attire a careful choice for tonight's movie premiere.

"You can't wear that jacket to the premiere," Mirabelle says, a mix of amusement and disbelief in her voice.

Caleb looks up in surprise. "Why not?"

"It looks like you're going bowling," Mirabelle responds, a smile playing at the corners of her mouth.

Caleb, taking a moment to consider her words, looks down. "This is my bowling jacket," he admits, a touch of pride in his voice, as if the jacket's association with leisure and enjoyment lends it a certain charm.

Mirabelle, catching his reflection in the mirror, allows herself a brief moment of amusement at the thought. "If you're suggesting that a bowling jacket is proper attire for a movie premiere, then I will be supportive," she offers, her words a blend of sarcasm and sincerity, an acknowledgment of their partnership's give-and-take.

Caleb, understanding the underlying message of support and acceptance in her words, feels a warmth spread through him. "That is all I have ever wanted," he says.

"The jacket or the support?" Mirabelle inquires, her tone light, laced with curiosity and a hint of amusement.

"Probably both," Caleb replies, his response tinged with a hint of humor and acknowledgment of the absurdity and affection inherent in their exchange.

A long pause ensues, filled with the rustling of fabric and the soft clinks of accessories being adjusted.

"We should be leaving soon," Mirabelle notes, her voice carrying a gentle urgency.

"We're waiting," Caleb states.

"What are we waiting for?" Mirabelle asks, her brows knitting in confusion.

"Tom is supposed to be taking us," Caleb reveals.

"I don't understand why Tom would take us to the premiere," Mirabelle expresses, her confusion evident.

"Tom picked me up from rehab and promised to take me to the premiere if we ever got the movie made," Caleb explains, a note of gratitude and proof of a deep-seated bond evident in his voice.

"I don't understand the relationship you have with him," Mirabelle confesses, her tone not one of judgment but of curiosity.

"He is kind of like my big brother. I have known him for longer than I can remember," Caleb responds, his words painting a picture of a relationship that transcends friendship, one that is rooted in a shared history—a bond that has provided him with guidance and support through the most challenging times of his life.

"It must be nice to have someone in your life like that."

"You have your brother."

"I did. He moved two years ago. He just came home one night and told me that he had to move to Seattle to start his life."

"How powerful...the power of Jack Reynolds. Well, maybe he'll find himself."

"I sure hope so. I worry about him."

"I worry about a lot of things in life. I worry from the moment I wake up until the moment I fall asleep, and then when I finally get to sleep, I worry about not being able to wake up," Caleb confides, revealing his own struggles with anxiety, a candid admission that opens up a window into his daily battles and the weight of the fears that accompany them.

"Have you mentioned this to your therapist?" Mirabelle inquires, her question not only an expression of concern but also a gentle nudge towards seeking support, recognizing the importance of professional guidance in navigating the complexities of such worries.

"It is weird that I tell you everything," Caleb confesses.

"It isn't weird. This is how relationships are supposed to work," Mirabelle responds, her voice imbued with conviction.

"No relationship I've ever been in," Caleb admits.

"Maybe that is why they have never worked," Mirabelle suggests.

The conversation then shifts with an outburst of frustration from

Caleb. "What if I just went without a tie? I mean, ties really aren't very 'hip.'"

"I have never heard you concerning yourself with 'hip,'" Mirabelle counters, her surprise evident.

"Everyone wants to be hip. Some people just hide it better than others," Caleb retorts.

"There are more ties on the rack, just try another one," Mirabelle advises, steering the conversation back to the immediate task at hand, her suggestion practical yet laced with an understanding of Caleb's underlying anxieties.

"This entire conversation is making me uneasy," Caleb confesses.

"It might be the tie," Mirabelle offers playfully.

"I think the tie is fine. I'm more concerned about seeing my own story on the big screen," Caleb reveals, getting to the heart of his anxiety. The prospect of his personal journey being portrayed in a movie, while an honor, is also a source of vulnerability and fear.

"It'll be fine," Mirabelle reassures him, her confidence intended to bolster Caleb's spirits, to offer him a sense of security amidst his apprehensions.

"How do you know?" Caleb questions, his doubt not just about the movie's reception but about the unpredictable nature of sharing one's life story with the world.

"Jack Reynolds has never been in a movie that was unsuccessful," Mirabelle points out.

"That just means he's due," Caleb counters.

Mirabelle's response to Caleb's apprehension about the movie's potential success—or lack thereof—is tinged with both *concern and playfulness.* "What a defeatist attitude," she chides.

"I'm just in touch with reality," Caleb counters, his defense a mixture of self-awareness and guarded cynicism born from past experiences.

"Is this how you're going to be all night?" Mirabelle probes.

"No, at one point I will get tired, then grumpy," Caleb replies.

"I don't know if I can handle you grumpy," Mirabelle confesses. Her words corroborate the depth of their connection, revealing a readiness to support and navigate the evening together, despite the emotional highs and lows that may come.

"Hold on. I have an idea," Caleb suddenly declares, a spark of inspiration cutting through the tension of the moment. He grabs a notepad and begins to scribble on it, his sudden burst of creativity a quality Mirabelle admires and sometimes finds inconvenient.

"You always have these fancy ideas at the worst times."

"When inspiration comes, the wise man seizes it," Caleb retorts. His response underscores a fundamental aspect of his personality—an openness to inspiration and a readiness to act upon it, regardless of timing or circumstance.

"I hope it doesn't take too long," Mirabelle responds. Her comment underscores the balance she seeks to maintain between supporting Caleb's creative impulses and ensuring that their evening proceeds smoothly.

"It takes as long as it takes," Caleb replies, his focus on the notepad unwavering. His dedication to the moment of inspiration, despite the practical considerations at hand, highlights his commitment to authenticity and expression, traits that Mirabelle, despite her reservations, ultimately respects and appreciates.

As Caleb continues to scribble, the doorbell rings. Mirabelle exits to answer it, returning with Heather.

"Look who decided to join us!" Mirabelle announces, her tone welcoming yet playful, as Heather's presence promises to add another layer of complexity and camaraderie to the evening.

"That jacket looks terrible on you, Caleb," Heather declares, her blunt assessment cutting through any pretense of politeness.

"That's what I've been telling him," Mirabelle concurs. The shared moment of consensus not only lightens the mood but underscores the importance of the relationships between Caleb, Mirabelle, and Heather—relationships built on honesty, support, and the shared anticipation of an evening that represents a significant milestone in Caleb's journey.

"Well, at least one of you has some taste in this house," Heather jests.

"I told him it looks like he's going bowling," Mirabelle says. The shared amusement over Caleb's jacket choice underscores the comfortable familiarity and gentle teasing that characterize their interactions.

"That is a spot-on critique," Heather concurs. The moment of levity serves to further bond Heather and Mirabelle, their shared perspective affirms their understanding and appreciation of each other's viewpoints.

"I'm glad you agree," Mirabelle responds. The exchange, light and filled with the warmth of friendship, momentarily sets aside the underlying tension and anticipation of the evening ahead.

Meanwhile, Caleb, engrossed in his sudden burst of inspiration, continues to scribble feverishly on the notepad. His focus is so intense that he seems momentarily disconnected from the conversation around him, his creative process a world unto itself within the shared space of the living room.

Heather shifts the tone of the conversation with an announcement. "Caleb, I come to you with some rather odd information," she begins.

"What is it?" Mirabelle inquires, her interest immediately captured by Heather's preamble.

"Who died?" Caleb asks.

"Wait, did someone die?" Mirabelle interjects.

Heather, recognizing the rising tension and potential for misunderstanding, clarifies, "I'm sure someone in the greater Los Angeles area did die, but..."

"I am more concerned with the written word than with whatever news you have," Caleb states.

Heather, concerned by Caleb's apparent indifference, questions, "Caleb, are you being dismissive?"

Mirabelle, better understanding Caleb's idiosyncrasies, interjects, "He gets this way when he's into what he's working on."

"What is he working on?" Heather asks.

"I never know," Mirabelle admits.

"It is of no concern until it is done," Caleb shouts from the other room.

"Don't mind him, Heather. What kind of news do you have?" Mirabelle asks.

"Yes, I did come here for a reason, didn't I?" Heather muses.

"Forget the reason behind my motivation," Mirabelle empathizes.

Heather, gathering her thoughts, delivers the unsettling news: "Well, apparently, last night, Jack was at a bar telling a young man about leaving Los Angeles, and the young man decided to beat him up and rob him."

"That's terrible," Mirabelle reacts, her empathy immediate, reflecting the gravity of the situation and its potential implications on their lives.

"Jack Reynolds is presently in the hospital, in a coma," Heather reveals.

"So, what does that mean for the premiere?" Mirabelle inquires. Her question is not one of insensitivity but rather an attempt to grapple with the cascading effects of this unforeseen tragedy on their professional and personal landscapes.

As the group contemplates the ramifications of Jack Reynolds' sudden hospitalization, Heather proceeds with pragmatism. "Well, unfortunately, the show must go on. We're just going to have to tell people that everything is fine," she declares, her statement reflecting a blend of industry savvy and the necessity of maintaining a façade of normalcy in the face of crisis.

Mirabelle, however, is quick to voice her concern, "But everything isn't fine." Her response underscores her empathy and her struggle with the ethical implications of concealing the truth for the sake of the premiere.

Heather's attempts to defuse the tension, "Where did you find her Caleb? She's cute," shifts the focus momentarily, drawing attention to Mirabelle's innocence or perhaps her idealism.

Caleb's reply, "The art beats out the movie star every time," serves as a cryptic endorsement of Mirabelle's stance, suggesting a deeper respect for the integrity of the creative process over the allure of celebrity. However, Mirabelle interprets Caleb's comment as insensitive, possibly because it seems to undermine the seriousness of their predicament.

Heather then offers a blunt assessment of the entertainment industry's transient nature, "For every movie star that steps away, there are a hundred more waiting to take their place," a statement that, while harsh, underscores the replaceability of individuals in the face of the industry's relentless momentum.

"So what happens now?" Caleb asks.

Heather immediately returns to the matter of Caleb's attire. "Well, the first thing you need to do is change that jacket," she insists.

Caleb stubbornly refuses. "I am not changing the jacket."

Heather's retort, "Well, at least wear a bag over your head," escalates the banter into a more pointed critique, her suggestion an exaggerated commentary on Caleb's defiance of conventional fashion standards.

"That's awful," Mirabelle interjects, her reaction indicating her discomfort with Heather's harsh humor, a reflection of her more sensitive nature.

"Not as awful as that jacket," Heather quips, undeterred.

"The jacket is a choice," Caleb affirms.

"Yeah, a terrible choice," Heather concludes.

Mirabelle, in an attempt to inject a note of optimism into the fraught atmosphere, reassures, "It will be fine. We will just go, and everything will be fine." Her words, though hopeful, carry an undercurrent of uncertainty, signaling her desire to believe in the best *possible outcome despite the complex emotions swirling around them.*

Caleb, however, can't help but question this optimism. "Or will it?"

"The word will get around," Heather interjects, *her statement vague yet laden with the implication that news of Jack's unfortunate situation will inevitably leak, becoming a topic of whispered conversations and speculation among their peers and the public.*

"What word?" Caleb asks.

"Choice," Mirabelle responds, *her answer a cryptic callback to their earlier conversation.*

"Are we talking about the jacket again?" Caleb queries, *slightly bemused.*

"I certainly hope not," Mirabelle replies, *her response indicating a desire to move past the trivial and focus on the more pressing concerns that loom over them.*

"Do you think he's going to pull through?" Caleb *shifts the conversation to the heart of their anxieties, voicing the question that has been hovering unspoken between them.*

"I certainly hope not," Heather says, *her response shocking in its apparent callousness. However, given Heather's previous interactions, this could either be a moment of dark humor misapplied, a slip of the tongue, or a profound misunderstanding of the gravity of the situation.*

Chapter 21

A DAY ON THE SET

The silence, complementing the early morning sky bathed in shades of pink in gold, was suddenly broken. Cameras buzzed intrusively, warming up for the long day ahead. The television program On the Set, which gained notoriety for its unreserved exploration of the wealthy and famous, was filming in a serene but surprisingly opulent rehabilitation facility, nestled away from the never-ending bustle of the adjacent metropolis. This episode, which focused on two unlikely friends—Fred Williams, whose voice had provided generations of radio listeners with solace, and Caleb Garcia, a novelist whose intricate tales had enchanted readers worldwide—promised to give viewers an unmatched look behind the scenes of recovery and redemption. Celebrated and examined equally, both men were caught up in a far-off spectacle that had little to do with their desperate attempts to find calm from their own storms.

The host of the show, Barry O'Donnell, was a character unto himself; he was well-known for taking advantage of celebrity weaknesses to increase audience engagement. Barry embodied the evil side of the entertainment world. His voice, dripping with a combination of feigned sympathy and undisguised greed for higher ratings, set the tone for what was to become an intrusive foray into personal healing. "Join us," he declared with a theatrical flourish, "as we venture into a journey seldom seen by the public eye, where the glitz and glamour of celebrity life fade into the background, leaving raw emotion and the struggle for recovery in their wake."

Caleb and Fred, both struggling with personal issues, arrived at the treatment facility with different goals in mind. Ever the optimist, Fred saw the participation as a chance to emphasize the significance of talking about mental health, particularly for public figures who frequently suffered in quiet. Under the mistaken assumption that the show may provide a significant platform, he aimed to highlight the difficulties of living in the spotlight and the vital importance of support networks. However, Caleb, who had a more pessimistic opinion of the media, saw the show as an inevitable evil. He was in a tight spot financially after the lackluster reception to his most recent effort, a film called Manchild, and the show's offer, disgusting as it was, saved him. However, neither man was quite ready for the looming invasion of their privacy.

The first few days were filled with a constant stream of cameras and incisive queries that were posed as worries. Barry's team, adept at manipulation, pushed Fred and Caleb to the edge of their emotions to get the most dramatic footage possible, hoping to seize every moment of vulnerability. Fred, who was used to steering his story via the radio, was finding it harder and harder to keep his cool, his normally composed manner breaking under the strain. Caleb, who was zealously guarding his private life, became more and more agitated, growing less patient with each intrusive question.

The friendship between the two suffered as a result of this unrelenting quest of sensationalism. What began as a shared experience and mutual understanding quickly turned into guarded exchanges as both guys learned to be wary of disclosing too much in front of the constantly monitoring cameras. Originally intended to be a place of healing, the rehab facility became a battlefield where people fought for their own space. Every moment of transparency was used as bait to boost the ratings of the show.

When they finally got their moment of privacy, free from the harsh light of the cameras, the actual nature of their situation became evident. One night, Fred and Caleb were on the center's terrace under the cover of darkness, with only the stars to light their way. Their shared experience had strengthened their bond beyond what the cameras were trying to capture.

Caleb admitted, "I never imagined it would be like this," his voice displaying obvious frustration. "It feels like we're trapped in a narrative we didn't choose, surrounded by walls we can't escape."

Fred gave a nod of assent, his features showing signs of weariness. "It's as if we're actors in a play written by someone else, forced to reveal our deepest fears for the world to see. I wanted to open up a conversation about mental health, but not at the expense of our own."

Fred and Caleb came up with a method to free their stories from the grip of sensationalism on that silent night of unity. In order to preserve the integrity of their treatment, they decided to put on a united front and only share the most routine parts of their voyage with the cameras. This subdued defiance of the story Barry was trying to force upon them was a turning point in their recovery.

As the days went by, Barry and his colleagues started to become frustrated with the lack of dramatic substance. The expected breakdowns and shocking disclosures did not occur; thus the show was unable to sustain its zeal for sensationalism. Barry's customary strategies proved futile when he saw Fred and Caleb's unshakeable resolve.

Barry O'Donnell was the archetypal example of a man whose career had thrived on the backs of others' personal hardships. He had perfectly styled, slicked-back hair, and an unceasing smile that seemed to be permanently etched on his face—a smile that, upon closer inspection, appeared never to truly touch the depths of his eyes. With the rehab center providing an odd backdrop for the day's filming, Barry's voice rang out in the cool early morning air, belied by *his genuine intents with a cold, planned tone of sympathy. He declared, his voice full of a fake warmth that sounded as genuine as it did hollow, "Today, we venture together into a realm rarely witnessed by the public eye." His announcement, intended to entice viewers with the promise of unguarded vulnerability, masked the exploitative nature of the endeavor, a fact not lost on those who knew to look beyond his charismatic presentation. "A journey beyond the glittering façade of celebrity, into a place where fame and fortune relinquish their hold, leaving only the raw and real struggle against personal demons."*

Caleb Garcia viewed the program with a much more realistic and skeptical perspective. The novelist had just experienced a setback in his career, despite his works once captivating the literary world. The lackluster reception to his most recent book (Manchild) had put him in a tight financial spot; he was facing the harsh realities of the publishing business. For Caleb, On the Set was a means to an end, a necessary concession to obtain the money required to maintain his livelihood and potentially support his future endeavors. While Fred was full of hope, he was cynical about the show's motives, and both men were caught off guard by the kind of manipulation and intrusion that was in store for them.

Caleb's pragmatism and Fred's idealism were put to the test when they set out on this expedition. Before long, the scenario they were in actually turned out to be very different from what they had anticipated. Their defenses were taken away by the show's intrusive cameras and sharp inquiries, which took advantage of their weaknesses for entertainment value. Fred was forced to walk a tightrope between sharing his experience and safeguarding his privacy as a result of the show's obsession with sensationalism, which undermined his hopes of encouraging important dialogues on mental health. Caleb, meanwhile, was forced to face the fact that he was a piece in a bigger game where people's personal problems were turned into commodities for television viewers, which validated his misgivings about reality television's exploitative character.

As the days went by, Fred and Caleb were forced to face not only their demons but also the moral dilemmas associated with taking part in a performance that preyed on human weakness due to the invasive nature of the production. The conflict between their original intentions and the actualities of their involvement in On the Set brought to light the intricate relationship between the need for private healing and the expectations of public consumption. Fred and Caleb set out on a voyage that would push the boundaries of their fortitude, alter their viewpoints on vulnerability and privacy, and ultimately transform their perception of the cost of being widely visible as they navigated this precarious balance.

Fred Williams and Caleb Garcia's first days inside the treatment facility, which was now transformed into a makeshift television set, passed in a blur of activity that was both unsettling and dizzying. The peaceful environment of their planned retreat was swiftly eclipsed by Barry O'Donnell's production crew, whose cameras and microphones became inconvenient fixtures in their day-to-day existence. During this time, a relentless stream of interviews that delved deeply into the most intimate details of their lives was conducted, ostensibly in the name of "transparency." However, this so-called transparency was nothing more than a blatant attempt at sensationalism, a carefully planned tactic to strip away the layers of their privacy in the hopes of striking television gold.

Under his direction, Barry's team showed an unwavering commitment to seize every instance of vulnerability, even at the expense of the people concerned. Their strategies were overtly obtrusive and intended to elicit strong feelings from their audience in exchange for engaging material. The goal of the production was to capture tears, breakdowns, or any other raw emotion that would guarantee a rise in the ratings. They pushed the men toward emotional extremes, navigating Fred and Caleb's complicated challenges with a ravenous desire for drama.

Although his radio background had polished his elegant and graceful communication style, Fred was at a loss for words in front of the camera's inflexible gaze. It became difficult to describe his recovery journey, which was paved with personal hardships and vulnerable moments. He felt a great deal of pressure to tell his story honestly and compellingly without giving in to hopelessness. His inability to remain composed under such intense scrutiny was evidence of the intrusive character of the show, which didn't seem to give a damn about its subjects' welfare.

Caleb, on the other hand, felt that the continuous questioning and observation went against his natural need for seclusion and his strong aversion to publicity. The very core of his existence shrank at the idea of having his private troubles exposed to the world. His tone hardened over the next few days, his answers to the production team's questions curter and more circumspect. There was a perceptible tension that replaced the once open and engaging discourse, a clear sign of his mounting discomfort and anger.

The dynamics between Fred and Caleb were significantly affected by this change in the center's atmosphere. Constant surveillance strained the camaraderie and mutual understanding that had begun to develop between them. Talks that used to be open and honest, providing comfort and empathy, turned defensive and contained. Each man grew more cautious about sharing too much information, conscious that every display of weakness may be turned into a story intended more for amusement than education.

The knowledge that their private moments of connection may

be used against them weakened their formerly harmonious relationship, which had the potential to be a source of strength and support. The fear of being revealed and having their words and feelings reinterpreted as entertainment value eclipsed any sincere moments of understanding and compassion that they may have had. The haven they had sought had indeed changed, but into a place where their weaknesses were not resources for recovery but rather features for amusement. They were now forced to negotiate the perilous waters of recovery while being mercilessly scrutinized by the public.

One night, on the balcony, away from the cameras, Caleb quietly said, "I didn't sign up for this," his voice colored with a mixture of resignation and frustration. His words echoed the sense of entrapment that had grown with each passing day, a feeling of being constantly watched, scrutinized, and judged, not just by the cameras but by an unseen audience eagerly awaiting their next moment of vulnerability. "I thought I could handle it," he continued, tone heavy with experience. "But it's everywhere. There's no escape."

As the night darkened and the stars attested to their predicament, Fred and Caleb had a chat that would prove to be crucial to their quest. Their realization that their participation in the show had deviated dramatically from their expectations and the aims they had planned to achieve led to a discourse of mutual understanding and shared commitment. The openness and vulnerability that would have offered support and healing had been tainted and turned into stories that suited the show's plot rather than the viewers' interests.

The atmosphere of the On the Set production became palpably tense as time passed within the rehabilitation center; that tension was only accentuated by Barry O'Donnell's mounting displeasure. The seasoned host, skilled at creating drama for the general public, was faced with an unanticipated obstacle when he realized that Fred Williams and Caleb Garcia would not bow to the sensationalism of reality television. Barry and his group created daily scenarios intending to elicit the kind of emotional turbulence and interpersonal turmoil that had come to define the program. However, every effort to weaken their unity or incite a breakdown was greeted with cool opposition and a measured reaction that left the production team at a loss for material.

It was now Barry, the host, who found himself in a situation he had not anticipated, necessitating a significant adjustment. For weeks, he had been ensconced in a whirlwind of anxiety and unyielding efforts, trying in vain to steer the narrative of On the Set toward the sensationalist tone that had initially catapulted the show to fame. However, as the series progressed toward its final episodes, there was a pivotal moment of surrender, marking the end of Barry's fruitless endeavors to mold Fred and Caleb's stories. This moment was not just a turning point for the show but a profound personal revelation for Barry, who recognized the futility of his attempts to exploit the genuine, raw experiences of his subjects.

Barry's decision to change the show's direction was met with a mix of surprise and admiration from the audience and critics alike. The viewers, who had initially been drawn in by the promise of drama and scandal, found themselves deeply moved by the authentic portrayal of resilience and recovery. The series evolved into a poignant narrative about the human spirit's capacity to triumph over adversity. Barry, through this transformative process, learned the value of authenticity over artifice, realizing that the most compelling stories are those that are told with honesty and empathy.

As the series concluded, Barry felt a sense of fulfillment he had not anticipated. He had embarked on this project intending to create *a hit show, but in the process, he had contributed to a narrative that offered hope and inspiration to many. The transformation of On the Set from a sensationalist reality show to a testament to human resilience and friendship was an accolade of Barry's growth as a director and storyteller. The final episodes served as a powerful reminder of the impact media can have in shaping perspectives and fostering a deeper understanding of the complexities of the human condition.*

The end of their tenure on On the Set signified a victory for Fred and Caleb that was far greater than any success in achieving high ratings. They had arrived as gullible spectators, featured on a show that would take advantage of their weaknesses for amusement. They came out on the other side not as victims of reality TV but as its masters. Their story served as a powerful reminder of the fundamental worth of upholding one's peace and dignity in the face of exploitation as well as the critical importance of solidarity in the face of public criticism.

Their involvement in the show left a legacy that was not one of dramatized hardships and televised upheaval, but rather one of human tenacity and the ability of individuals to create their own narratives, even when working within the confines of a reality television format. Under the constant scrutiny of the cameras, Fred and Caleb's rehabilitation path had evolved from a potentially vulnerable spectacle into a story of empowerment and self-determination.

The final hour of On the Set had arrived, bringing with it a tangible sense of finality and introspection. Caleb and Fred found themselves seated in an empty office, the remnants of their time on the show packed neatly into the bags at their feet. The room was silent except for the soft hum of the air conditioning, a stark contrast to the hustle and bustle that had characterized their days on set. As they awaited their departure, the weight of the moment settled upon them, prompting a conversation that would seal their friendship in a promise for the future.

Fred broke the silence first, his voice carrying a mix of nostalgia and determination.

"Caleb, can you believe it's already over? Feels like we just got here, and now we're about to step back into the real world."

Caleb nodded; his gaze fixed on the bags. "Yeah, it's surreal." His gaze lifted to Fred's. "I wanted to say...thank you for sticking with me. We did this together. I couldn't have done it alone...I could use a friend like that out there, too, you know?"

Fred smiled; the sentiment echoed in his own heart. "Same here, man. We've seen each other at our worst and best. It's not something you forget or let go of easily."

There was a pause as both men considered the gravity of their shared experiences. Caleb then spoke, his voice firm with resolve. "I want to make a promise, Fred. No matter where we go from here, we've got to support each other. We've been through the fire, and we know what's at stake. I don't want to ever let go of this friendship. It's been a lifeline, and I believe we can keep being that for each other, even outside of this place."

Fred extended his hand, a gesture of solidarity and commitment. "I'm with you, Caleb. We've fought hard to get to this point, and I'm not about to let distance or time weaken what we've built. You've got my word, brother. We'll check in on each other, keep pushing forward, and be there when it counts. We've seen how easy it is to fall, but now we also know how to help each other stand back up."

Caleb clasped Fred's hand; the pact sealed between them. "And let's not forget the laughter, man. We've had some good times amidst the chaos. It's that balance that's going to keep us sane."

Fred laughed, the sound a balm to the solemnity of their conversation. "Absolutely. The world's too grim without a good laugh. We'll keep those coming too."

As they stood up, bags in hand, they shared a look of mutual respect and understanding. The journey they had embarked upon in On the Set had been unexpected and fraught with challenges, but it had also forged a bond that would extend far beyond the confines of the show.

"We've got this," Caleb said, a smile spreading across his face.

"Absolutely," Fred replied. "Together, there's nothing we can't handle."

With that, they stepped out of the empty office, not just as friends but as brothers in arms, ready to face whatever the world had in store for them. As Tom waved to Caleb from a limousine, and Fred walked toward an Uber, they knew their friendship was a beacon that would guide them through the darkest of times. The show was over, but their story was just beginning.

Chapter 22

THE PREMIERE OF PAPERWEIGHT

The city lights blurred into streaks of neon, casting a kaleidoscopic glow over the sleek black limousine as it wove its way through the bustling streets of downtown. Inside, Caleb and Mirabelle were cocooned in a world far removed from the chaos outside, a bubble of anticipation and nerves. The air inside the car was charged with a palpable energy, a heady mix of excitement and the weight of the moment that lay ahead. Seated comfortably yet restlessly, Caleb found himself lost in thought, his mind a whirlpool of memories and emotions tied to the journey that had led him to this night. Mirabelle, ever the calming presence, sat beside him, her hand finding his in the dim light, offering silent support and understanding.

Tom was the embodiment of professionalism and care, his attention divided between the road ahead and his client. He glanced from the window to Caleb in a moment of silent communication. His smile, meant to be reassuring, was tinged with a tension that mirrored Caleb's own internal turmoil. Despite the veneer of calm, there was a sense of shared anticipation, a collective understanding of the significance of this event.

"We're almost there," Tom's voice broke through the quiet, a gentle reminder of the approaching climax of their journey. He adjusted his tie in the mirror, a small gesture that betrayed his nerves. "Remember, Caleb, breathe. This is your night." His words, simple yet profound, were meant to ground Caleb, to remind him of the enormity of the achievement they were about to celebrate. It wasn't just any premiere; it was the unveiling of Paperweight, a film that bore Caleb's soul to the world, a narrative woven from his darkest days and his journey to redemption.

The limousine turned a corner, the neon lights giving way to the floodlit façade of the theater, a guiding light in the pitch-black night drawing them closer to the moment of truth. The anticipation inside the car crescendoed, a tangible force that seemed to envelop them. Caleb took a deep breath, Tom's advice echoing in his mind, trying to steady the storm of emotions that threatened to overwhelm him.

As the car slowed to a stop, Caleb felt the pulsating energy of the crowd waiting outside, the flash of cameras, the press of bodies—all of it awaited him just beyond the safety of the limousine's tinted windows. This was the moment of transition, from the private struggles of his past to the public acknowledgment of his journey. It was unequivocal proof of his resilience, a story of falling and rising, of losing oneself and finding a path back to the light.

Mirabelle squeezed his hand tighter, a wordless gesture of solidarity and encouragement. They were in this together, partners in life and in this moment of vulnerability. Tom's presence, too, was a source of strength, a reminder of the professional support that had helped guide Caleb to this point. Together, they formed a circle of support, ready to face the lights, the cameras, and the eyes of the world.

As the door opened, spilling light into the darkened interior of the car, Caleb took one last breath, steeling himself for the onslaught of attention. This was his story, his life, laid bare for the world to see. And as he stepped out into the night, greeted by the roar of the crowd and the blinding flash of cameras, he realized that this was more than just his night. It was a celebration of survival, of the power of the human spirit to overcome, to heal, and to emerge stronger on the other side.

As the limousine glided to a graceful halt in front of the venue, the night air was instantly alive with the cacophony of excitement and anticipation. The venue itself was a spectacle, bathed in the glow of spotlights that cut through the darkness, illuminating the red carpet that stretched like a ribbon of honor toward the grand entrance. The atmosphere was charged, a tangible buzz of anticipation that seemed to vibrate through the very ground. Cameras flashed like lightning in a summer storm, capturing every moment, every movement, with the voracity of those hungry for the story behind the spectacle. The murmur of the crowd swelled, a sea of voices rising and falling with the excitement of the evening. They had gathered in droves, fans and onlookers, their eyes all turned toward the sleek black vehicle that held inside it the man of the hour and his companion.

Tom, ever the professional and guardian of his charge, was the first to emerge from the limousine, his figure cutting a dashing silhouette against the backdrop of lights and expectant faces. He extended a hand back into the vehicle, a gallant gesture meant to assist Mirabelle as she made her entrance. Dressed in a gown that seemed to capture the very essence of elegance, Mirabelle stepped into the night, her presence commanding the immediate attention of all who beheld her. The gown, chosen with meticulous care, was a light cream color, and it clung and flowed in all the right places, a revelation of her grace and the thoughtfulness with which she approached this momentous occasion.

Following closely behind, Caleb emerged from the cocoon of the limousine wearing what was earlier described as a "hideous" bowling jacket. He felt a weight born of anticipation, vulnerability, and the silent fear that accompanies the baring of one's soul. Yet, as he stepped into the limelight, he bore that weight with a sense of duty and pride. The air around him was electric, charged with the energy of those gathered to witness the unfolding of a story that was deeply personal, yet universally resonant. The moviegoers craned their necks for a better view, their eagerness palpable. The press, armed with cameras and microphones, jostled for position, all vying for the chance to capture a word, a glance, a moment of vulnerability from the man whose life's trials and triumphs were about to be laid bare on the silver screen.

As Caleb made his way along the red carpet, each step felt significant. The crowd's murmurs, the incessant flash of cameras, the captivating atmosphere—all of it merged into a backdrop for a moment that was at once deeply personal and profoundly public. This was not just any film premiere; this was a pilgrimage, a journey to the heart of a story that had seen the darkest nights and the brightest dawns. The anticipation of the moviegoers and the eagerness of the press were but reflections of the broader human experience, a collective yearning for stories that move, challenge, and inspire.

The red carpet beneath his feet felt like a bridge between two worlds—the world of his past, with its shadows and trials, and the world of his present, where those very trials were being transformed into a message of hope and resilience. With Mirabelle by his side, a symbol of unwavering support and love, and Tom leading the way, a shining example of professional guidance and assurance, Caleb walked forward, each step an assent to the journey that had brought him here. The air, charged with anticipation, seemed to pulse with the collective heartbeat of those gathered, a symphony of human connection that underscored the significance of the night. This was more than a film premiere; it was a celebration of survival, a testament to the power of redemption and the unyielding strength of the human spirit.

As Caleb and Mirabelle made their way along the red carpet, a figure emerged from the flurry of activity, a calm presence in the whirlwind of excitement and anticipation that enveloped the event.

Heather, the producer behind the cinematic journey of Paperweight, approached with a demeanor that seemed to part the sea of people. Her arms were open, a gesture of welcome and camaraderie, as she moved toward them with grace.

"Caleb, Mirabelle," Heather greeted. The sincerity in her tone, the genuine warmth that radiated from her, was a balm to the undercurrent of nerves that accompanied such a monumental evening. "Thank you for being here tonight," she continued, her words carrying the weight of gratitude and respect. "This film...it's going to change lives, Caleb. Your courage in sharing your story is going to resonate with so many."

The journey down the red carpet transformed with Heather's presence, her words a reminder of the significance of the night. For Caleb, each step became a reflection, a tangible link to the journey he had undertaken from the darkest corners of addiction to this pinnacle of achievement. The surreal quality of the moment enveloped him, the red carpet beneath his feet a ribbon through time that connected his past with his present, each step a milestone that marked the distance he had traveled. Cameras captured every moment, their flashes punctuating the night like stars, while voices called out his name, a chorus that acknowledged his journey and the bravery it took to share it with the world.

Yet, amidst the spectacle and the acclaim, Caleb's focus remained fixed on the doors that stood at the end of the carpet, the grand entrance to the theater that loomed ahead like a portal to a new realm. These doors represented more than just the physical entry to a building; they were the gateway to a new chapter in his life, a threshold that, once crossed, would mark the transition from his past to his future. The anticipation of what lay beyond, of the shared experience of witnessing his story unfold on the silver screen, lent a gravity to his steps. It was as if each footfall was a heartbeat, a rhythm that carried him forward, propelled by the knowledge that what awaited was a culmination of his journey, a moment of triumph born from the ashes of his darkest days.

The red carpet became a chasm or path that led not only to the premiere of a film but to a moment of validation and recognition. This was not just his story; it was a testament to the resilience of the human spirit, a narrative that promised hope to those still ensnared in the throes of addiction, a beacon of light that signaled the possibility of redemption and renewal. As he neared the doors, the anticipation of the audience inside, the collective empathy and understanding that would greet his story, filled him with a sense of purpose. This was his moment of triumph, not just a celebration of his own journey, but an offering of hope to others, a shared experience that would, as Heather had promised, resonate with so many.

Upon entering the theater, Caleb, Mirabelle, and their companions were enveloped by an atmosphere thick with anticipation. The air itself seemed to hum with the collective excitement and nervous energy of the audience, a palpable force that reverberated with the significance of what was about to unfold. As they made their way to their seats, the murmurs and whispers of the gathered crowd blended into a backdrop of sound, an intimation of the draw of the story that was soon to be shared. Caleb's heart beat a frantic tempo, the culmination of years of struggle, pain, and eventual triumph about to be laid bare for all to see. This wasn't just another movie premiere; it was a public unveiling of his most private battles, a narrative spun from his own experiences with addiction and the arduous path to recovery.

Mirabelle, ever attuned to Caleb's emotional state, took his hand in hers, her grip firm yet gentle, a silent demonstration of her unwavering support. This simple act, the warmth of her hand enveloping his, served as an anchor, a reminder of the strength and love that had supported him through the darkest times and into the light. It was a physical manifestation of the bond they shared, one forged in the fires of adversity and strengthened by mutual respect and devotion.

As the theater lights began to dim, signaling the start of the film, a hush fell over the audience, the anticipation reaching its zenith. The opening scenes burst onto the screen, a visceral portrayal of Caleb's past life, depicted with an unflinching honesty that immediately captured the audience's attention. The images, the sounds, the very essence of his former existence were laid out in stark relief, a mirror to the reality he had once lived. Caleb found himself caught in the grip of the film, each scene a reminder of the journey he had undertaken, from the depths of despair to the hard-won fight for redemption.

Jack Reynolds enveloped the character of Caleb with a raw intensity that would eventually be recognized as his legacy performance. It would in fact be a still shot from the film that would eventually be played in his In Memoriam for the academy.

It was as if the filmmakers had peeled back the layers of Caleb's life, exposing the vulnerability, the pain, and the sheer willpower that defined his struggle. He watched, mesmerized, as his own story was reflected back at him, each scene testifying to the trials he had endured. The experience was emotional, a rollercoaster that plunged him back into the depths of his past before ascending into the light of his present.

Throughout the film, Mirabelle's presence was a constant source of comfort. Her hand, steadfast in his, was a lifeline, a tangible reminder that he was no longer alone in his journey. Her support was unwavering, her belief in him unshakable. This shared experience, watching his life story unfold on the big screen, served to reinforce the bond between them, a connection that had been tested by the trials of addiction and strengthened by the journey toward recovery.

As scene after scene played out, Caleb was acutely aware of the audience around him, their reactions a mirror to his emotional journey. The film did not shy away from the harsh realities of addiction, nor did it gloss over the monumental effort required to reclaim one's life from its grasp. It was a story of hope, of the possibility of redemption, and of the power of love and support to overcome even the darkest of times.

Caleb's journey, so intimately portrayed on the screen, was a testament to the human spirit's capacity for resilience, a narrative that spoke to the heart of every viewer. The experience of watching his life story unfold, framed by the comfort of Mirabelle's presence and the collective empathy of the audience, was a cathartic release, a final step in the process of healing and acceptance. It was a moment of vulnerability, of exposure, but also one of immense pride and gratitude for the journey that had brought him to this point.

As the narrative arc of Paperweight reached its poignant conclusion, the atmosphere within the theater shifted palpably. The final scenes, a powerful declaration of the resilience of the human spirit and the redemptive power of change, unfolded on the screen, leaving a tangible silence in their wake as Caleb (Jack Reynolds) left the rehab facility with open scars on his arms and face. The audience, so captivated by the raw honesty and emotional depth of Caleb's story, remained in a collective hush, as if holding their breath, fully immersed in the gravity of what they had witnessed. The weight of Caleb's journey, from the depths of despair to the heights of redemption, lingered heavily in the air, a shared emotional burden that connected each person in the room.

Then, as the last image faded and the credits began to roll, the theater was suddenly alive with movement. It started with a *few, then dozens, and soon the entire audience was on their feet, a wave of spontaneous applause that crescendoed into a thunderous ovation. This was no ordinary acknowledgment of cinematic achievement; it was a heartfelt recognition of the courage it took for Caleb to share his story, of the struggle he endured, and of the redemption he ultimately found. The applause echoed, a resounding tribute that filled the theater, a chorus of admiration and respect that seemed to say, without words, "We see you, we honor your journey, and we are moved by your strength."*

For five unbroken minutes, the applause continued, a tangible manifestation of the audience's deep connection to the story they had just witnessed. It was an outpouring of emotion, a communal celebration of Caleb's bravery, his vulnerability, and his triumph over adversity. The sound filled every corner of the theater, an overwhelming symphony of recognition that resounded the very essence of human empathy and solidarity.

Within this sea of acclaim, Caleb stood, visibly moved, tears welling in his eyes as he took in the scene around him. The emotional weight of the moment was palpable, a culmination of years of struggle, pain, and ultimately, healing. As he looked around, he saw the faces of the crowd, each one reflecting the impact of his story. Tom, his agent and steadfast supporter through the highs and lows of his career, beamed with a pride that was both professional and deeply personal. Heather, the visionary producer who had believed in the power of Caleb's story to inspire and transform, wiped away joyful tears, her emotion an endorsement of the profound effect the film was already having.

And then there was Mirabelle, the woman who had stood by him through the darkest times, whose love and belief in him had been unwavering. Her eyes met his, shining with tears of joy and pride, a silent communication of love, support, and shared victory.

Her presence, both in his life and in this moment, was his anchor, a reminder of the power of love to heal, to support, and to triumph over the worst of circumstances.

This standing ovation, this moment of collective acknowledgment, was more than just applause for a film; it was a celebration of human resilience, of the capacity for change, and of the incredible journey that Caleb had embarked upon. It was a moment of connection, of shared humanity, and of the transformative power of storytelling. For Caleb, it was a validation of his decision to share his story, an affirmation that his journey could inspire hope, encourage empathy, and perhaps even change lives. Amid the applause, surrounded by the people who had supported him, believed in him, and now celebrated him, Caleb felt a profound sense of gratitude, closure, and hope for the future.

This extraordinary evening, unfolding within the grandeur of the theater, transcended the typical glitz and glamour of a movie premiere. It morphed into a profound affirmation of Caleb's harrowing yet inspiring journey, serving as a vibrant exposition of the boundless power of hope and the indomitable resilience of the human spirit. The relentless applause that reverberated through the space was not merely a gesture of appreciation for cinematic achievement; it was a resonant acknowledgment of the depth of struggle, the courage in vulnerability, and the strength found in redemption that Caleb's story exemplified. This night became a beacon, shining brightly not just for Caleb, but for every soul entangled in their battles, whispering promises of light even in the darkest of times.

As the applause washed over him, a continuous wave of sound and emotion, Caleb stood enveloped in a moment of transcendence. This wasn't just about the accolades or the recognition of his personal narrative; it was a communal embrace, a collective understanding that stretched beyond the confines of the theater.

Paperweight, while undeniably rooted in Caleb's experiences, had blossomed into a universal message, a clarion call to those wrestling with their demons in the solitude of their shadows. It was a narrative that said, unequivocally, that no one is alone in their struggles, that the journey through darkness can lead to light, and that redemption, though fraught with challenge, is within reach.

Caleb, amidst the thunderous applause, found himself at the heart of a profound realization. This journey, his journey, had evolved into a beacon of hope for others, a lighthouse guiding lost ships through tumultuous seas to the safety of the shore. The message of Paperweight served as a powerful reminder that darkness is not the end, that healing is possible, and that every step taken towards the light, no matter how small, is a victory. It was a message of solidarity, of the strength found in unity and in the shared belief that tomorrow can be brighter than today.

In this moment of overwhelming recognition and support, Caleb understood the true impact of his story. It was a catalyst for conversation, a bridge connecting isolated islands of struggle, and a source of comfort for those who felt unseen and unheard. The film, and by extension, this night, symbolized a collective journey toward understanding, acceptance, and healing. It was a celebration of the human capacity to overcome, to find beauty in brokenness, to emerge stronger from the crucible of adversity.

As the applause finally began to ebb, Caleb was left with a profound sense of gratitude and purpose. This experience, this affirmation of his journey, had not only marked a personal milestone but had also illuminated a path for others. Paperweight was more than his story; it was a shared narrative of hope, resilience, and redemption, a reminder that no one is alone in their journey through darkness. And in that realization, Caleb found not just closure, but a renewed commitment to being a beacon in the lighthouse of life, guiding others home to a place of understanding, acceptance, and peace.

Chapter 23

THE PLIGHT OF HEATHER

Heather, the esteemed president of Mangold Films, found herself navigating a scenario vastly different from the luminous allure of film premieres and the strategic confines of polished executive boardrooms. Here she was, ensconced within the modest back office of Bill's Drug Store, a setting more familiar with the hum of fluorescent lights than the sparkle of Hollywood. The office was a compact space, cluttered with the essential paraphernalia of the pharmacy trade: shelves laden with medical supplies, a desk strewn with paperwork, and filing cabinets filled with patient records. The stark contrast to her usual work environment was palpable, with the clinical scent of antiseptics mingling with the mustiness of paper, a world away from the perfumed ambiance of movie sets and high-powered meetings.

Opposite her, William stood firmly, embodying the role of the pharmacist with every fiber of his being. With his arms folded and a look of measured skepticism etched across his features, he regarded Heather with a mix of curiosity and wariness. His life had been dedicated to the health and well-being of his community, deciphering the often-inscrutable handwriting of doctors, and providing counsel and care to those who walked through his pharmacy's doors. The notion of engaging in discussions that veered towards the cinematic was as foreign to him as the idea of a pharmacist leading a boardroom meeting would be to Heather.

"What exactly are you suggesting, Heather?" The question hung in the air, voiced by William with a skeptical yet curious tone. It was clear William was a man not easily influenced by the superficial charm or persuasive tactics that might sway others in different

circles. His life's work, rooted in the tangible realities of healthcare and medicine, had imbued him with a pragmatism difficult to penetrate. Years of experience honed his ability to assess situations with a critical eye, ensuring the health and safety of his customers were never compromised. Yet, in this moment, faced with an offer that lay beyond the bounds of his everyday experiences, William found himself navigating uncharted waters.

Heather, fully aware of the unusual nature of her request and the environment she found herself in, knew she had to approach the conversation with tact and sincerity. The leap from managing a successful film production company to negotiating in the cramped quarters of a drug store back office was significant, yet it substantiated her dedication to authenticity and her willingness to explore unconventional avenues for her projects. Mangold Films, under her leadership, had always prided itself on pushing the boundaries of storytelling, seeking out real-world locations that added depth and realism to their cinematic endeavors.

In the face of William's evident disbelief, Heather understood that winning him over would require more than the usual industry talk. It would necessitate a genuine connection, an assurance that her interest in his pharmacy was rooted in a respect for his profession and a belief in the value his authentic experience could bring to her film project. This was not merely a business transaction; it was an invitation to collaborate, to bridge the gap between two vastly different worlds with the shared goal of creating something impactful and resonant.

The dialogue that ensued between Heather and William, in the unlikely setting of the drug store's back office, illuminated the power of storytelling, the potential for unexpected connections, and the magic that can arise when open minds converge. Heather's journey into William's domain, a detour from the glitz of Hollywood *to the grounded reality of pharmacy work, underscored the lengths to which she was willing to go to ensure the authenticity and integrity of her film projects. For William, the encounter presented an opportunity to view his everyday world through a new lens, to see the value in his work and life experience as contributing to a narrative larger than the sum of its parts.*

Heather, with her extensive experience as a seasoned negotiator and executive in the cutthroat world of film production, was acutely aware of the delicate nature of this particular dialogue. Her position as president of Mangold Films had often placed her in high-stakes negotiation scenarios, yet the current setting—a cramped, paper-strewn back office of a community drugstore—presented a unique challenge that diverged significantly from her norm.

"William, I understand how this situation may appear somewhat unconventional to you," Heather initiated. "But I assure you, the intentions behind our presence here today are rooted in authenticity and a genuine interest in your establishment. We're in the process of scouting locations for an upcoming project. It's a low-budget film, but it carries a narrative that's deeply embedded in the fabric of everyday life, focusing on a community pharmacy that serves as a cornerstone for its neighborhood—a setting not unlike your own here."

William's reaction to Heather's explanation was a mixture of curiosity and a lingering skepticism, a natural response given the unusual nature of the proposition laid before him. The furrow of his brow eased slightly as he considered her words. "And why, may I ask, did you choose to embark on this...interrogation, for lack of a better term, within the confines of my back office?" he queried, the choice of 'interrogation' imbued with a light, almost playful tone that hinted at his warming demeanor.

Heather, perceptive to the changing tide in William's attitude, seized the opportunity to further elucidate her purpose and, hopefully, cement a newfound rapport. "The decision to meet here, in the heart of your operations, wasn't made lightly," she continued. "It stems from a belief in the importance of authenticity and a desire to understand the true essence of the environment we aim to replicate on screen. Your pharmacy, with its rich history and integral role within the community, offers a perspective that could greatly enrich our narrative. This is not about merely using your space as a backdrop but integrating its genuine character into the fabric of our film."

William listened, the initial reservations he harbored beginning to dissipate as the potential impact and significance of what Heather proposed became clearer. The notion that his everyday world—the pharmacy he had dedicated years of his life to, cultivating relationships with the community, and navigating the complexities of the healthcare system—could play a central role in a film project was both flattering and intriguing. The idea that the authenticity of his work and its significance to the community could be highlighted and appreciated on a broader scale presented an unexpected opportunity, one that transcended the routine of daily prescriptions and patient consultations.

Heather's smile broadened. "Indeed, William, this isn't an interrogation in the traditional sense," she clarified, her tone light yet earnest, aiming to further soften the edges of their meeting. "Think of it more as an exploratory conversation about a unique opportunity. In our quest to find the perfect setting for our next film project, we've visited numerous locations, yet none have struck us with the same sense of authenticity and community spirit as your store. Moreover, your expertise and daily experiences as a pharmacist offer a depth of insight that could prove invaluable to the success of our narrative."

William shifted his posture, leaning back against the edge of his cluttered desk with a thoughtful expression. "I see," he mused. "And what exactly would this 'opportunity' entail for me?"

Seizing upon William's engagement, Heather leaned in, her demeanor animated by the burgeoning potential of the moment. Her proposal was bold, yet she delivered it with a contagious enthusiasm that illuminated her vision for the project. "How would you feel about stepping into the world of cinema, William?" she proposed, her voice tinged with excitement and anticipation. "Imagine not only serving as a consultant, providing us with the invaluable legitimacy of your professional perspective, but also playing a role in the film as the pharmacist. It's a small part, but one that could add a significant layer of realism and depth to the story. And beyond the contribution to the film, it's an opportunity for a unique and memorable experience. Imagine the story you'd have to share, the blend of your real-world expertise with the magic of movie-making."

William's eyebrows rose. "Me? In a movie?" The question echoed in the cramped back office, bouncing off walls lined with pharmaceutical supplies and paperwork, creating a momentary bubble of surrealism within the ordinary setting. The notion seemed so drastically out of sync with the reality of his day-to-day life—a life dominated by the methodical rhythm of managing prescriptions, advising patients, and navigating the complexities of healthcare—that it verged on the fantastical. Yet, as William observed the sincerity and enthusiasm in Heather's gaze, a spark of curiosity began to ignite within him, challenging the boundaries of his daily existence.

The routine that had once defined his professional fulfillment—the predictability of the pharmacy, the familiar faces of his regular customers, the steady flow of medical inquiries and health concerns—had gradually evolved into a landscape of repetition.

The contours of his world had become too well-trodden, too familiar, leaving him with a quiet yearning for something new, something that would disrupt the monotony and inject a dose of unpredictability into his life. Heather's unexpected proposition, therefore, struck a chord, presenting an enticing gateway to an experience entirely outside the field of his professional expertise and personal expectations. Here was a chance to venture beyond the well-defined parameters of his pharmacy, to partake in an adventure that promised to weave elements of his real-world knowledge into the fabric of a cinematic narrative.

After a moment of contemplation, punctuated by the internal weighing of pros and cons, William's response emerged, marked by a shift in demeanor. His initial skepticism melted away, replaced by a burgeoning sense of possibility. A grin, uncharacteristic of his usual reserved expression, began to spread across his face, softening features that were more accustomed to conveying professional assurance than spontaneous amusement. "Well, Heather," *he said,* "I suppose it wouldn't hurt to add 'movie star' to my resume, even if it's just a small part."

Heather, attuned to the nuances of human expression and the subtle indicators of interest, recognized the significance of William's response. Beneath the playful tone and the casual framing of his acceptance was a clear indication of his willingness to embrace this unexpected opportunity.

"Excellent!" *Heather's exclamation reverberated through the small, cluttered back office of Bill's Drug Store, her voice a mixture of triumph and relief. The path that had led her to this moment was as unexpected as it was fortuitous. She had embarked on what she assumed would be a straightforward mission to secure a location for Mangold Films' next project, never imagining that she would find herself deep in negotiation within the confines of a pharmacy's back office. The idea of not only negotiating location permissions but also casting the pharmacist himself in a role within the film had seemed implausible. Yet, as the conversation with William unfolded, what had initially appeared to be a detour transformed into a serendipitous opportunity. The sense of accomplishment Heather felt was not just from securing a unique setting for the film but from bridging two seemingly disparate worlds, bringing a fresh, authentic element to the storytelling process.*

As they ascended the specifics of the arrangement, the atmosphere in the room shifted palpably. The initial tension, born of uncertainty and skepticism, gradually melted away, replaced by a burgeoning sense of camaraderie and mutual excitement about the project. William, who had spent years within the familiar confines of his pharmacy, attending to the needs of his community, found himself viewing his everyday environment through an entirely new lens. The prospect of his pharmacy serving as a backdrop for a story, of his daily sphere of prescriptions and patient care being transformed into a cinematic setting, ignited his imagination. The mundane aspects of his surroundings took on a new significance as he envisioned the transformation that would take place, turning the familiar setting of his drugstore into a vibrant movie set.

By the time Heather stepped out of Bill's Drug Store and back into the wider world, she carried with her the satisfaction of having secured not just a unique location for Mangold Films' upcoming project but also an unexpected addition to the cast. William, the pharmacist, with his genuine demeanor and deep-rooted connection to the community, had become an unlikely yet invaluable asset to the film. The encounter served as a potent reminder of the rich mélange of stories and characters that existed beyond the traditional confines of the film industry. It underscored the truth that compelling narratives and characters often lay hidden in plain sight, waiting to be discovered by those willing to look beyond the conventional and embrace the richness of real-life experiences.

Not only did Heather and William's fortuitous partnership show how much power comes from being open, creative, and fearless in exploring unexplored territory, but it also vividly proved that the most meaningful stories and genuine characters are frequently born from the most unexpected encounters. This experience reinforced Heather's belief in the fundamental principle that storytelling was about more than just making up stories; it was about capturing the genuine and diverse range of human experience. It showed her how important it was to maintain an open and curious mindset when she was creating. In contrast, William's entry into the world of cinema was about to bring an unprecedented chapter to his life story, radically altering his perspective on his work and the influence he has in the larger context of his community.

Filmmaking is as much an adventure into uncharted territory and meetings with unique characters as it is about the stories themselves, and the collaboration between Mangold Films and Bill's Drug Store is a powerful symbol of the unexpected intersections of art and everyday life. In the end, what started as Heather looking into the pharmacy as a possible location for filming turned into a team effort that aimed to bring some real-life magic to the world of cinema. It proved again and again that the essence of storytelling is connected to a desire to discover, make connections, and fully embrace the boundless possibilities that life offers.

Chapter 24

HOW WE RESOLVE

After a career that shone under the relentless spotlight of celebrity, Caleb's life was about to take a drastically different turn as his career came to an end. As a sad reminder of a bygone era, the shouts that had formerly accompanied his every stride now echoed gently in his mind. Substance abuse, which had a devastating effect on his life, had finally broken its grip. The affection he had fought so hard to avoid instead nurtured a serene acceptance.

Up until this point, his journey had been anything but smooth sailing, full of hazards and dangerous cliffs that could have swallowed him whole. There was a time when the hypnotic attraction of fame served as a compass for him. But the limelight started to fade with the years, exposing its shadows in his life. Once a symphony of love, the applause now resounded like a mournful echo, revealing the hollowness behind his glittering exterior. He had become much lonelier, more entangled than before due to his addiction, a relentless enemy that had lied to him about freedom and pleasure.

Love, an emotion he had always regarded with suspicion and caution, started to cast its soft light onto him when he was at his lowest point of despair. With unfaltering compassion and support, Mirabelle stood beside him. Her presence had been a steady, though much disregarded, light in his life. Her devotion, in contrast to the transient praise from his admirers, was genuine and unwavering, a refuge from the turbulent waves of his turmoil. She helped Caleb view himself as a redeemable human being, rather than the tarnished celebrity he had become due to his troubles and controversies.

He found solace in Mirabelle's affection, which anchored him in her unfaltering faith in his ability to overcome his addiction and the inner demons he was fighting. In the depths of his soul, away from the prying eyes of the media, he waged this war, where the full breadth of his affliction was exposed. Reclaiming the fragments of his identity that had been shattered by years of being in the spotlight felt like fighting for his fundamental core.

The road to recovery was bumpy and winding. Every day presented new obstacles, uncertainties, and temptations that could have derailed Caleb's journey. But the weight of his past and the shackles of addiction began to slip away as he made progress. Mirabelle's love served as a continual inspiration for him to rise above the devastation and face the future.

After enduring the ups and downs of stardom, addiction, and love, Caleb came to a profound realization—his value was not measured by the praise and admiration of outsiders, but by the deep bonds he formed with people who genuinely cared about him. His once-strained relationship with Mirabelle flourished again as a result of their shared resilience, openness, and honesty, free from the constraints of his public persona.

Caleb realized, as he stepped across the starting line of this new chapter, that the renown he had always desired no longer possessed much appeal. More valuable than any praise or prize was the love he had discovered in Mirabelle and in accepting himself. Caleb entered the future, free from the shackles of his past, envisioning a world where love, not celebrity, would determine his lasting impact.

Caleb found the will to beat his addiction and the bravery to accept love at its most basic level in this tranquil place. Living a life of genuine purpose, unencumbered by the weight of others' expectations, he could finally let the echoes of acclaim fade into the background and be replaced with the peaceful serenity that comes from truly belonging somewhere and accepting himself just the way he was.

As Caleb set sail on his perilous expedition, he encountered hazardous waters. The entire idea of hope appeared like an elusive mirage. Despite every move, hopelessness loomed huge, casting a darkness so thick that light seemed a terrible fiction. The depths of despair were the very places where the first sparks of love could be seen breaking through the whole blackness. Staying at his side was Mirabelle, who had unfaltering belief in Caleb's potential. She loved him with an unassuming optimism that guided him away from the rocky shores of gloom. Her love was a symbol of her peaceful strength. A ray of light in the chaos, this love was unfussy and based on the truth of their shared path, not some idealized version of happily ever after.

A deep understanding came to Caleb as he walked the lonely road to recovery. Like the ephemeral beauty of a sunset, the charm of celebrity was temporary and, in the end, deceiving. The hunt ended at the horizon, where the spotlight's warmth and adoration gave way to the twilight's icy apathy. Addiction is a silent war that rages in the depths of the spirit, and he knew that no amount of public praise or approval could win that conflict. In order to triumph, he had to face the ghosts of his past, guided by the light of self-awareness and strengthened by the love and encouragement of the few courageous people who stuck with him through the worst of times.

This conflict did not take place on a great platform, and neither were its triumphs celebrated with ovation. Rather, it developed during Caleb's reflective times, as he battled to accept and acknowledge the aspects of himself from which he had long wished to create distance. When everything else in his life seemed hopeless, Mirabelle was more than just a friend; she was his rock. A continual reminder of the man he wanted to be, rather than the darkness that addiction had cast, was her faith in his ability to overcome the demons that plagued him.

He found direction in his life's work after realizing that stardom was just a mirage. Once the bedrock of his existence, the praise and the devoted followers were now dwarfed by the real relationship and unvarnished love Mirabelle provided. Caleb discovered redemption in this love, which did not necessitate the façades of fame, or a life lived in the limelight. Rather, it pleaded for honesty, for the bravery to accept and even celebrate his flaws.

The long road to rehabilitation taught Caleb to look at himself through Mirabelle's eyes instead of the world's—as a man of value, able to change, and worthy of love. Deep periods of self-doubt, haunted by memories of failed attempts and the constant worry of relapsing, were hallmarks of this path of self-discovery and development. However, as he progressed, the shackles of his addiction began to slip, and he was embraced by a love that demanded nothing less than his authentic self.

The ordeal ultimately transformed Caleb into a new man. Suddenly, the notoriety that had shaped his sense of self appeared like a little thread in the fabric of his existence. He would be remembered more for the struggles he overcame within, the love he let himself experience, and the light he brought to those who were still struggling after he had emerged from the shadows, than for the novels he sold or screenplays he had sold. By accepting Mirabelle's love, Caleb discovered a way to find forgiveness and came to understand that the most significant triumphs are achieved in private, away from public scrutiny.

With Mirabelle's hand firmly intertwined in his, Caleb strolled *through the streets he had never been before, thinking back on the stormy road that had brought him to this peaceful acceptance. He had a profound epiphany when he realized that the glory he had sought could not be attained by public acclaim or stardom, but rather through the legacy of change he would bring about. This legacy signified a change from the story that had previously characterized his life; it was a testimony to the unbreakable bond between people, the triumph of love over addiction, and the hollow sound of praise. Despite his past struggles with addiction and trauma, his story arrived at a happy ending, one marked by positive love and redemption. It was love that saved him from his lowest point.*

Instead of the perfect world Caleb had imagined, he felt the inner peace that comes from accepting one's own shortcomings and finding love in that acceptance. During this introspective trip, Caleb discovered what celebrity truly is. He understood that it was more important to consider the effect one has on those they care about than to base one's worth on public perception. Looking beyond the fleeting light of praise and toward a lasting impact, this change of viewpoint shed light on the way ahead.

As they walked, Caleb's past and present intertwined; the streets he had used for performances, that had housed his demons, now provided the setting for his new story. Every stride he took was a symbol of the fight for his soul and the path to self-discovery. Thanks to Mirabelle's unwavering support and the courage he gained during his worst moments, his struggles with addiction, which had earlier been fought in the spotlight, had evolved into triumphs of personal development.

The enormous size of the bond between Caleb and Mirabelle became more obvious as they traversed the world together, no longer as onlookers but as companions in a common quest for salvation.

A profound, reciprocal comprehension of one another's hardships and achievements, rather than the transient passions of fame or the empty trappings of celebrity, formed this relationship. They had found refuge in each other's love and acceptance as they had weathered the tempestuous waters of Caleb's addiction.

This love had shone like a lighthouse in the night, leading Caleb to his deliverance. Nothing was required of the lover, so long as the recipient was ready to face their deepest anxieties and weaknesses. Thanks to Mirabelle's unfaltering encouragement, Caleb realized that the fight isn't for external praise but for inner peace, and that the real fight is often waged inside.

Caleb discovered refuge from the storms of his past and a light for his future in the serenity of this understanding. His story, once seen as a cautionary tale about addiction and stardom, was now being rewritten as one about love's transformational power, resilience, and optimism. The sound of acclaim grew fainter as they pressed on in their shared trip, but the serenity and assurance that come from knowing you've made a difference were ever-present. Here, in this post-performance society, Caleb realized that the true measure of fame was not in material success but in the impression, one makes on the people they hold dear—a legacy of lasting friendships, shared experiences, and the power of love to overcome overwhelming odds.

Chapter 25

CURTAIN CALL

Michael stood in the dimly lit wings of the Seattle theater, his heart pounding like the rhythm of a distant drum. Tonight marked the grand opening of "Julius Caesar," and he, in the role of the eponymous character, was at the epicenter of the performance's impending brilliance. His sister, Mirabelle, a steady presence by his side, radiated unwavering support and encouragement, having flown in from Los Angeles just to witness his moment of triumph.

"You're going to be magnificent tonight, Michael," she whispered, her voice a soft melody in the cacophony of backstage preparations.

Michael offered a grateful smile, his nerves tingling with anticipation. Mirabelle's belief in him was a beacon of strength, grounding him amidst the storm of emotions swirling within.

As the call for places echoed through the theater, Michael took a deep breath, centering himself in the moment. Weeks of meticulous preparation had led to this juncture—each line memorized, every gesture refined, until he embodied the essence of Julius Caesar himself.

The curtains ascended, revealing the stage bathed in ethereal light. Michael stepped forward, his presence commanding, his voice resonant with the weight of centuries. With each word, he wove a tapestry of intrigue and betrayal, drawing the audience deeper into the heart of ancient Rome.

As the play unfolded, Michael surrendered himself to the character, channeling Caesar's pride, his ambition, his inexorable fate. With every step, every gesture, he breathed life into the legendary leader, immersing himself in the role with an intensity that bordered on transcendence.

As the pivotal moment of Caesar's assassination approached, Michael felt a surge of adrenaline course through him. With bated breath, he braced himself for the inevitable, his senses heightened, his emotions raw and unbridled.

The stage erupted into chaos, the echoes of betrayal reverberating through the air. In that fleeting instant, Michael became Caesar—defiant, betrayed, immortalized in tragedy.

As the final curtain descended, the theater erupted into a symphony of applause, a testament to the power of Michael's performance. Basking in the adoration of the audience, he felt a profound sense of accomplishment wash over him, a validation of his craft and dedication.

Backstage, amidst the camaraderie of his fellow cast members, Michael shared the news with Mirabelle, his eyes ablaze with excitement.

"I've been offered a role in Jack Reynolds' new film," he revealed, his voice tinged with disbelief and elation. "It's a story about an orphan who saves his home by staging a play about Julius Caesar."

Mirabelle's eyes widened in awe, her pride for her brother palpable. In that moment, as they stood bathed in the glow of his success, Michael knew that the journey ahead held infinite promise, fueled by his passion for acting and the unwavering support of those who believed in him.

Meanwhile, in Los Angeles, Mirabelle's husband Caleb, a screenwriting professor at USC, eagerly awaited her return. They had been married for a year, their love blossoming amidst the bustling streets *of the city of angels. As Mirabelle shared the news of Michael's success over the phone, Caleb couldn't help but feel a swell of pride for his brother-in-law, knowing that greatness awaited him on the silver screen.*

ABOUT THE AUTHOR

Stephen McGill stands out as a distinguished veteran of the US Army, celebrated for his unwavering service to his country and his impactful contributions to the technology and storytelling spheres. Married to his partner Andria for nearly a decade, Stephen's seamless transition from military service to a leadership role in the Information Technology sector is a testament to his resilience, versatility, and relentless pursuit of excellence. Upon his honorable discharge, he ventured into the vibrant world of information technology, quickly establishing himself as a seasoned IT Program Manager. His substantial military background has equipped him with extraordinary leadership skills and a deep understanding of team dynamics, essential qualities that have propelled him to the forefront of successful IT project management.

Beyond his professional achievements, Stephen is a passionate advocate for the transformative power of storytelling in all its forms. He is deeply committed to the idea that stories have the unique ability to forge connections, impart wisdom, and reflect the myriad experiences of humanity. His interests span from immersing himself in classic literature to exploring the latest in science fiction series and crafting his own stories. This belief not only enriches his personal life but also influences his approach to leadership and teamwork, promoting an environment of innovation, empathy, and profound insight into the world.

Stephen McGill's narrative is marked by his dedication to service, remarkable leadership, and love for the stories that bind us together. His journey, enriched by his partnership with Andria and his deep personal passions, showcases the power of dedication, expertise, and the continuous search for meaningful connections and significance.